Primary Language Arts

Grade 2

NSC Edition

Diana Anyakwo
Heather Raymond
Mitzie-Ann Jackson

The Publishers would like to thank the following for permission to reproduce copyright material.

Photo credits

p.14: © spotmatikphoto/stock.adobe.com; p.15 (tl) © mavoimages/stock.adobe.com, (tr) © Daniel Ernst/stock.adobe.com, (bl) © spotmatikphoto/stock.adobe.com, (bc) © Samuel B./stock.adobe.com, (br) © pololia/stock.adobe.com; p. 16: © InsideCreativeHouse/stock.adobe.com; p. 21: (tl) © LIGHTFIELD STUDIOS/stock.adobe.com, (tr) © Farinoza/stock.adobe.com, (cl) © Eric Isselée/stock.adobe.com, (cr) © hhelene/stock.adobe.com, (bl) © lms_lms/stock.adobe.com, (br) © Eric Isselée/stock.adobe.com; p.41: (t) © New Africa/stock.adobe.com, (cl) © Bokeh Art Photo/stock.adobe.com, (cr) © Olexandr/stock.adobe.com, (c) © Coprid/stock.adobe.com, (bl) © V.R.Murralinath/stock.adobe.com, (br) © Andrzej Tokarski/stock.adobe.com; p.45: (t) © Roman Samokhin/stock.adobe.com, (tr) © Анна Бортникова/stock.adobe.com, (cl) © LIGHTFIELD STUDIOS/stock.adobe.com, (cr) © terex/stock.adobe.com, (bl) © Günter Albers/stock.adobe.com, (br) © courtyardpix/stock.adobe.com; p.61: (tl) © pixelrobot/stock.adobe.com, (tc) © alter_photo/stock.adobe.com, (tl) © Alexstar/stock.adobe.com, (br) © Farinoza/stock.adobe.com, (bc) © Mara Zemgaliete/stock.adobe.com, (br) © terex/stock.adobe.com; p. 68: © Aksinia/stock.adobe.com; p. 86: (t) © Aksinia/stock.adobe.com, (c) © Happy monkey/stock.adobe.com, (b) © filmlandscape/stock.adobe.com; p. 100: © Petr Toman/Shutterstock; p.112: (t) © Julydfg/stock.adobe.com, (bl) © Scanrail/stock.adobe.com, (bc) © cristi180884/stock.adobe.com, (br) © rod5150/stock.adobe.com; p.116: (tl) © NDABCREATIVITY/stock.adobe.com, (tc) © olly/stock.adobe.com, (tr) © WavebreakMediaMicro/stock.adobe.com, (bl) © onephoto/stock.adobe.com, (br) © Prostock-studio/stock.adobe.com; p.118: (t) © Aksinia/stock.adobe.com, (l) © mipan/stock.adobe.com, (c) © Alekss/stock.adobe.com, (c) © Fyle/stock.adobe.com, (cr) © Mara Zemgaliete/stock.adobe.com, (r) © lucielang/stock.adobe.com; p.119: (tl) © Ken Hurst/stock.adobe.com, (tr) © pololia/stock.adobe.com, (c) © Aksinia/stock.adobe.com, (tl) © Digital Storm/stock.adobe.com, (tr) © Alex Kondratenko/stock.adobe.com; p.120: (t) © Aksinia/stock.adobe.com, (b) © Sergey Novikov/stock.adobe.com; p.122: © bestphotostudio/stock.adobe.com; p.123: (tl) © PF-Images/stock.adobe.com, (tr) © Eric Hood/stock.adobe.com, (cl) © vladakela/stock.adobe.com, (cr) © Liaurinko/stock.adobe.com, (b) © Chirawan/stock.adobe.com; p.124: © cunaplus/stock.adobe.com, (r) © Tatty/stock.adobe.com, © azure/stock.adobe.com, © Adam Nowak/Wirestock/stock.adobe.com, © T Rose/peopleimages/stock.adobe.com, © nerthuz/stock.adobe.com; p.131: (tl) © kmiragaya/stock.adobe.com, (tc) © gamelover/stock.adobe.com, (tr) © Samuel B./stock.adobe.com, (bl) © iofoto/stock.adobe.com, (bc) © Anatoliy Karlyuk/stock.adobe.com, (br) © Gelpi/stock.adobe.com; p.144: © Nikola Spasenoski/stock.adobe.com, © Adam Nowak/Wirestock/stock.adobe.com, © zhu difeng/stock.adobe.com, © BillionPhotos.com/stock.adobe.com, © koya979/stock.adobe.com, © Ban/stock.adobe.com, © nerthuz/stock.adobe.com, © Paul/stock.adobe.com, © Coprid/stock.adobe.com, © Catmando/stock.adobe.com, © cunaplus/stock.adobe.com, © Liza/stock.adobe.com, © Kletr/stock.adobe.com; p.163: (tl) © alfa27/stock.adobe.com, (tr) © BoBloob/stock.adobe.com, (bl) © Lukas Gojda/stock.adobe.com, (br) © Eric Isselée/stock.adobe.com, (bl) © lukyee_nuttawut/stock.adobe.com, (br) © Rawpixel.com/stock.adobe.com; p.174: (tl) © siwarug/stock.adobe.com, © Aksinia/stock.adobe.com, (br) © Glamy/stock.adobe.com; p.183: (tl) © Romolo Tavani/stock.adobe.com, (tcl) © Sascha Burkard/stock.adobe.com, (tcr) © Syda Productions/stock.adobe.com, (tr) © lowsun/stock.adobe.com, (bl) © cunaplus/stock.adobe.com, (bcl) © intra/stock.adobe.com, (bcr) © amorn/stock.adobe.com, (br) © Sumala/stock.adobe.com; p.185: (l) © tomas/stock.adobe.com, (cl) © wavebreak3/stock.adobe.com, (c) © jonnysek/stock.adobe.com, (c) © Prostock-studio/stock.adobe.com, (cr) © lovelyday12/stock.adobe.com, (r) © banphote/stock.adobe.com; p.186: © pressmaster/stock.adobe.com; p.189: © Siphosethu/peopleimages/stock.adobe.com; p.202: © cunaplus/stock.adobe.com, © AlenKadr/stock.adobe.com, © nerthuz/stock.adobe.com, © alanmc67/stock.adobe.com, © pachaileknettip/stock.adobe.com, © Prostock-studio/stock.adobe.com, © Eric Isselée/stock.adobe.com; p.203: (t) © Happy Monkey/stock.adobe.com, (c) © rawintanpin/stock.adobe.com, (b) © Eric Isselée/stock.adobe.com; p.204: (t) © Vladimir Melnik/stock.adobe.com, (c) © New Africa/stock.adobe.com; p.236: © Sony Herdiana/stock.adobe.com, © Syda Productions/stock.adobe.com, © compuinfoto/stock.adobe.com, © boophuket/stock.adobe.com, © Maria/stock.adobe.com, © David/stock.adobe.com, © Amelia Fox/stock.adobe.com, © Africa Studio/stock.adobe.com, © Atlas/stock.adobe.com, © Krakenimages/stock.adobe.com, © M Einero/peopleimages.com/stock.adobe.com, © cunaplus/stock.adobe.com; p.253: © Media Lens King/stock.adobe.com; p.258: © conzorb/stock.adobe.com; p.259: (t) © nikkytok/stock.adobe.com, (c) © Gajus/stock.adobe.com; p.274: © Debbie Ann Powell/stock.adobe.com, © Leon718/stock.adobe.com, © Harris Shiffman/stock.adobe.com, © Wangkun Jia/stock.adobe.com, © Giongi63/Shutterstock, © Craig F Scott/Shutterstock, © Giongi63/stock.adobe.com, © ajlatan/stock.adobe.com; p.280: (tl) © lucky-photo/stock.adobe.com, (tr) © Mark James/stock.adobe.com, (bl) © azureus70/stock.adobe.com, (br) © EdNurg/stock.adobe.com; p.281: © Marius Igas/stock.adobe.com; p.310: © K Davis/peopleimages/stock.adobe.com; p.312: © MAITREE/stock.adobe.com, © lordn/stock.adobe.com, © michaeljung/stock.adobe.com, © mipan/stock.adobe.com, © Denis Feldmann/stock.adobe.com, © Krakenimages/stock.adobe.com, © Rido/stock.adobe.com, © Ivan Kmit/stock.adobe.com, © Sviatoslav Kovtun/stock.adobe.com, © VIEWVEAR/stock.adobe.com, © malija/stock.adobe.com, © wavebreak3/stock.adobe.com, © 3dmitry/stock.adobe.com.

Although every effort has been made to ensure that website addresses are correct at time of going to press, Hodder Education cannot be held responsible for the content of any website mentioned in this book. It is sometimes possible to find a relocated web page by typing in the address of the home page for a website in the URL window of your browser.

Hachette UK's policy is to use papers that are natural, renewable and recyclable products and made from wood grown in well-managed forests and other controlled sources. The logging and manufacturing processes are expected to conform to the environmental regulations of the country of origin.

To order, please visit www.hoddereducation.com or contact Customer Service at education@hachette.co.uk / +44 (0)1235 827827.

ISBN: 978 1 3983 5290 2

© Diana Anyakwo, Heather Raymond, Mitzie-Ann Jackson and Hodder & Stoughton Limited 2024

This edition published in 2024 by

Hodder Education,

An Hachette UK Company

Carmelite House

50 Victoria Embankment

London EC4Y 0DZ

www.hoddereducation.com

Impression number 10 9 8 7 6 5 4 3 2 1

Year 2027 2026 2025 2024

All rights reserved. Apart from any use permitted under UK copyright law, no part of this publication may be reproduced or transmitted in any form or by any means, electronic or mechanical, including photocopying and recording, or held within any information storage and retrieval system, without permission in writing from the publisher or under licence from the Copyright Licensing Agency Limited. Further details of such licences (for reprographic reproduction) may be obtained from the Copyright Licensing Agency Limited, www.cla.co.uk

Cover illustration by Heather Clarke c/o D'Avila Illustration Agency

Illustrations by Heather Clarke c/o D'Avila Illustration Agency and Hyphen S.A.

Typeset by Hyphen S.A.

Printed in Spain

A catalogue record for this title is available from the British Library.

Contents

Contents..3

Term 1 **Unit 1**

Chapter 1 10

Speaking and listening: Greet each other; play a game; ask and answer questions in Jamaican Creole and Standard Jamaican English 10

Word builder: Vocabulary of Jamaican place names; list names in alphabetical order; identify sounds in words; identify and pronounce *b* and *p* sounds in words....................... 12

Let's read: Read a non-fiction, descriptive text; answer questions; complete sentences adding missing word; complete a family tree 14

Grammar builder: Present tense form of the verb "to be"; identify correct usage in sentences 16

Let's write: Write sentences about yourself following question prompts..................... 17

Chapter 2 18

Speaking and listening: Take turns to ask and answer questions; talk about personal experience; do a class survey and report back to the class... 18

Word builder: Write names in alphabetical order; match words and pictures with same sound; play a letter game using alphabetical order 20

Let's read: Read a poem; identify rhyming words; answer questions 22

Grammar builder: Use personal pronouns in sentences 24

Let's write: Use descriptive vocabulary and question prompts, write about and draw your friend; write a rhyming poem about a friend 26

Chapter 3 29

Speaking and listening: Use picture cues to tell a story; use sequencing words; add a further section and tell it to others; ask and answer questions about your story 29

Word builder: Recite the alphabet; write 10 place names in alphabetical order; differentiate long and short vowel sounds; complete simple words with missing vowels; identify rhyming words... 31

Let's read: Read a descriptive text; answer questions; talk about what you have read 33

Grammar builder: The past tense of the verb "to be" in the third person; change sentences from present tense to past tense; write sentences in the past tense 34

Let's write: Use question prompts to interview a partner; draw and write about their response; use past tense of the verb "to be"; use correct personal pronouns................................... 35

Chapter 4 36

Speaking and listening: Talk about the days of the week and the months of the year; identify first and last letter sounds in words; talk about own experience, using sentence prompts.. 36

Word builder: Focus on the *th* sound, differentiating between voiced and voiceless sounds; write and spell the months of the year 37

Let's read: Read a calendar and answer questions 39

Grammar builder: First, second and third person pronouns; singular and plural pronouns...40

Let's write: Make a calendar, drawing rows and columns, writing days, months and dates; write in special school events and holidays on the correct dates 41

Chapter 5 43

Speaking and listening: Listen to and identify Jamaican Creole and Standard Jamaican English words; listen to a song; compare JC and SJE versions of a song; read or sing the song in JC; transcribe the song into SJE 43

Word builder: Match rhyming words with pictures; identify rhyming words; spell simple words following a rhyming pattern 45

Let's read: Predict a story from picture cues; read a story and suggest missing words; identify repeated patterns of sounds or words 47

Grammar builder: Plural nouns; write plural forms for simple words 49

Let's write: Think and talk about songs; write an additional verse for a song; use patterns and rhymes in writing 51

Chapter 6 52

Speaking and listening: Use pictures to predict and tell a story; tell a story using sequence words; listen to a story 52

Word builder: Identify and define words from the story; identify rhyming words 53

Let's read: Read a story using picture cues; put sentences in correct sequence to tell a story; match speech bubbles to characters; role play a story in groups 54

Grammar builder: Present and past tense of the verb "to be"; write sentences using verb "to be"; identify correct use of verb tense; introduce past continuous tense 57

Let's write: Introduce story structure and setting; write a story using a story starter and story planner 59

Term 1 Unit 1 Review and assessment... 61

Term 1 | Unit 2

Chapter 7 65

Speaking and listening: Role play a conversation about taking turns; express a view; play a game 65

Word builder: Identify long and short vowel sounds; add "magic e" to words; match words to pictures 67

Let's read: Read a text, identify and correct spelling mistakes; answer comprehension questions 69

Grammar builder: Past tense verbs with regular endings; sound endings of past tense verbs; use capital letters, full stops and commas 71

Let's write: Create a picture as a writing stimulus; use planning questions to draw a monster; write descriptive sentences about your drawing 73

Chapter 8 74

Speaking and listening: Work in groups of three to draw a picture; discuss the picture; agree a story about it; present to class, speaking in order; describe process of developing story, using starter sentences and sequencing words 74

Word builder: Identify long and short vowel sounds 76

Let's read: Read a text; identify regular past tense verbs; answer comprehension questions; complete sentences; identify words with long vowel sounds and silent final "e"; identify words from their definitions 78

Grammar builder: Complete sentences using past tense verb form; differentiate between different sounds in word endings; complete sentences with correct word 81

Let's write: Plan a piece of writing about an accident which has happened; use the past tense; draw a picture of the accident; write about the accident using vocabulary box and questions; make sure story has beginning, middle and end; read and check 82

Chapter 9 84

Speaking and listening: Take it in turns to mime a word or sentence for your partner to guess; develop mimes together to show to other students 84

Word builder: Identify rhyming words; match rhyming words to pictures 86

Let's read: Read a text and answer questions; introduction to character description 87

Grammar builder: Change sentences from present to past tense; write sentences using past tense; correct punctuation in sentences 89

Let's write: Write a letter to a friend; use question prompts; use an outline plan 91

Chapter 10 92

Speaking and listening: Listen and respond to instructions; work in teams to play a game in which imagined objects are described; ask and answer questions; mime actions 92

Contents

Word builder: Identify rhyming words; spell simple rhyming words; add "magic e"/"silent e" to words 93

Let's read: Read and discuss a story; make notes describing the main characters; ask and answer questions about the characters; relate story to own experience, reflect and discuss 95

Grammar builder: Use past tense verbs to complete sentences; find and correct spelling and grammar mistakes in sentences 97

Let's write: Plan and write a report 99

Chapter 11 100

Speaking and listening: Take turns to read aloud and ask questions; match title with text 100

Word builder: Identify context clues in writing/artwork; locate information in a text; answer questions using information in the text 102

Let's read: How to read information in a table format; study and answer four types of comprehension question: "right there", "think and search", "author and you" and "on your own" 104

Grammar builder: Past tense forms of regular verbs; identify final sounds of past tense verbs; complete a table showing spelling and sounds of past tense verb endings; write sentences using past tense verbs 106

Let's write: Work in groups to plan, research and write about a sporting hero; complete an information table; plan and write three sequenced paragraphs 108

Chapter 12 110

Speaking and listening: Work in groups to plan a presentation based on the "Let's write" exercise in Chapter 11; share tasks among the group; structure the presentation with beginning, middle and end; deliver presentation to class 110

Word builder: Talk about common IT items; match words to definitions 112

Let's read: Read a text and answer questions 113

Grammar builder: Identify past tense verb forms in text; use past tense verbs in sentences; complete sentences with correct past tense verb; identify regular and irregular past tense verb forms 115

Let's write: Use question prompts and time expressions to write a story about an event in the past 117

Term 1 Unit 2 Review and assessment 118

Term 2 Unit 1

Chapter 13 121

Speaking and listening: Take turns reading a poem aloud; reflect on and talk about personal responses to the poem; describe sensory experiences such as eating an orange; ask and answer questions about personal experience 121

Word builder: Look at consonant blends; match words to images; identify correct letter patterns 123

Let's read: Identify and discuss similes in a poem; read a poem and draw a picture about it; compare two poems; analyse similes; write a simile 125

Grammar builder: Construct questions using the verbs "to do", "to have" and "to be"; sort sentences into correct order to make questions; complete questions with correct words 127

Let's write: Work in groups to plan and write a poem; use similes to describe feelings and senses 129

Chapter 14 131

Speaking and listening: Listen to a text about body language and give presentations; discuss aspects of body language 131

Word builder: More work on blended consonants; identify correct consonant blend to complete words; identify consonant blend to match pictures 134

Let's read: Predict text from picture clues; add missing words to complete a rhyming poem; talk about a poem, expressing personal responses 136

Grammar builder: Add "-ed" to form the past tense of regular verbs; rewrite sentences with capital letters and correct punctuation 138

Let's write: Describe the main characters in a story of your choice; explain the structure of the story – beginning, middle (what happens) and end; write the story using the past tense; read part of story to class 140

Chapter 15 142

Speaking and listening: Role play conversations in different settings; ask and answer questions; in pairs research and talk about a figure in Jamaican culture; discuss your figure with other class members 142

Word builder: Identify consonant blends *sh*, *ch*, *th*, *ph*; read and discuss a poem; identify consonant blends at the beginning, middle and end of words 144

Let's read: Predict texts from title and opening sentence; answer comprehension questions on a text; answer *true* or *false* questions 146

Grammar builder: Complete a table; use "-ed" form in past tense verbs; write negative sentences; select "a" or "an" before words 148

Let's write: Plan and write a story on Jamaican history, using a graphic organiser; identify characters and story structure; write in the past tense 151

Chapter 16 152

Speaking and listening: Ask and answer questions using picture stimulus; relate to own experience; discuss and compare experiences; show appreciation 152

Word builder: Homophones; complete sentences using correct word 153

Let's read: Read a non-fiction text and answer comprehension questions 155

Grammar builder: Identify the subject in a sentence; identify the verb in a sentence; identify and write complete sentences 157

Let's write: Choose a celebration and discuss ideas with a partner; draw or make a picture of the celebration; answer questions using complete sentences; write about the event 159

Chapter 17 161

Speaking and listening: Take turns to read a poem aloud; role play the actions in the poem as you read; ask and answer questions about birthdays; express and justify a point of view 161

Word builder: Identify homophones; match correct words to pictures; select correct word to complete sentences 163

Let's read: Read an invitation; obtain information from an invitation; introduce RSVP protocol .. 165

Grammar builder: Identify the subject in a sentence; identify noun or pronoun as sentence subject; use pronouns correctly in a sentence 167

Let's write: Write an invitation using appropriate vocabulary; use sentence starters to structure an invitation 169

Chapter 18 170

Speaking and listening: Take turns to read a text aloud; draw a response to the text; ask and answer questions; speak from own experience 170

Word builder: Introduce homographs; match words with definitions; complete a story using a selection of homographs correctly 171

Let's read: Read a poem; revisit similes; devise similes for the five senses 173

Grammar builder: Use correct pronouns; add correct capitalisation/punctuation to a paragraph of text 175

Let's write: Work in groups to study poetic form; write a sentence about each of the five senses; write a short poem about the senses and read it aloud 177

Term 2 Unit 1 Review and assessment 179

Term 2 Unit 2

Chapter 19 183

Speaking and listening: Ask and answer questions using picture stimulus; express an opinion 183

Word builder: Break words into syllables; identify different syllables within words; match words and pictures 185

Let's read: Read a blog and answer questions; identify specific information in text.................. 186

Contents

Grammar builder: Proper nouns; review sentences and correct punctuation; solve anagrams 187

Let's write: Use picture stimulus and starter sentences to write a story in the past tense ... 189

Chapter 20 191

Speaking and listening: Put pictures in correct sequence order; take turns to describe the life cycle of a plant, using sequence words; research information about a plant and make a presentation to the class.......................... 191

Word builder: Play a word game, matching word sounds; say and spell words; identify words spelled verbally 193

Let's read: Read a non-fiction text about the lifecycle of tomato plant; answer comprehension questions 194

Grammar builder: Plural forms of regular and irregular nouns; use commas and full stops in sentences 196

Let's write: Identify the verb tense in a text; choose a plant and research it; write about the life cycle of the plant using starter sentences 198

Chapter 21 200

Speaking and listening: Look at pictures and listen to a story; answer questions; role play one of the pictures for others to guess; mime the nouns 200

Word builder: Identify silent letters in words; complete crossword puzzle using words with silent letters.. 202

Let's read: Read texts, match headings to text; answer questions on the text................... 203

Grammar builder: Plural forms of regular and irregular nouns; add correct punctuation to sentences 205

Let's write: Plan a piece of writing using stimulus ideas; draw a picture; write about your drawing 207

Chapter 22 209

Speaking and listening: Look at pictures and listen to the story; ask and answer questions about the story using question words; discuss the story and express an opinion 209

Word builder: Speak words aloud and categorise by spelling/sound; identify *ou* and *ow* sounds; write sentences using *ou* and *ow* words 210

Let's read: Read a story; match words to their meanings; answer comprehension questions; reflect on story and express an opinion; discuss characterisation 211

Grammar builder: Identify past tense verbs in a text; identify correct form of past tense verbs; complete sentences with past tense verbs....... 214

Let's write: Talk about stories and choose one to write about; use prompts to structure the story; draw pictures and write the story........................ 215

Chapter 23 216

Speaking and listening: Read a speech; ask and answer questions; work in groups to plan a speech on a selected theme; share the work so everyone participates; deliver the speech to the class.. 216

Word builder: Link syllables to form words; identify number of syllables in words 218

Let's read: Read a non-fiction text; answer *true* or *false* questions.. 219

Grammar builder: Use a double consonant in past tense form of verbs 220

Let's write: Write a report; plan and make a model and write a report of the process including title, description of process, materials used and the results 222

Chapter 24 224

Speaking and listening: Read instructions on making a model; choose an item to make; draw and write the instructions on a poster; give a presentation to the class using the poster... 224

Word builder: Identify words with silent letters; identify and spell words containing the *oi/oy* sound 226

Let's read: Read and follow instructions 228

Grammar builder: Present continuous case; use the present continuous form of the verb "to be" in sentences; complete sentences with the correct verb form; write questions using the present continuous; review formation of sentences using the past continuous................ 230

7

Let's write: In groups decide what to make using recycled materials; write the instructions 234

Term 2 Unit 2 Review and assessment 236

Term 3 | Unit 1

Chapter 25 240

Speaking and listening: Read and sing a traditional song; ask and answer questions.... 240

Word builder: Vowels followed by "r"; "-er" ending on words; use a spelling wheel 242

Let's read: Read short texts and select missing titles; answer comprehension questions........... 244

Grammar builder: Work with simple sentences; use the word "and" to make plural subject; use sentence starters to make simple sentences with plural subjects; use adjectives 246

Let's write: Choose adjectives to describe a place you know; write a paragraph describing a specific place and say why you like it............. 248

Chapter 26 249

Speaking and listening: Role play a conversation between a market stall holder and a customer; use sentence starters to write and role play another conversation 249

Word builder: Identify voiced and unvoiced sounds; count syllables in words 251

Let's read: Read and role play a conversation; answer questions 253

Grammar builder: Singular and plural subject pronouns; select pronouns for given sentences; differentiate between subject and object pronouns; identify adjectives in sentences....... 254

Let's write: In groups, plan and write a conversation in a market; role play the conversation for the class.................................... 257

Chapter 27 258

Speaking and listening: Read advertisements; ask and answer questions; identify persuasive language 258

Word builder: Recognise and identify synonyms; list adjectives and find synonyms 260

Let's read: Predict text from pictures; read text; find adjectives and synonyms; answer questions; link text to own experience and reflect 261

Grammar builder: Use possessive pronouns 263

Let's write: Read a letter and identify correct pronouns; use letter as model to write a letter in reply.. 264

Chapter 28 265

Speaking and listening: Read a poem and answer questions; read aloud; identify and express response to poem; relate to own experience.. 265

Word builder: Vowels followed by "r"; words ending "-er", "-or", "-ir" and "-ar"; pronounce and spell the different endings 267

Let's read: Predict text from picture; read descriptive text; express a view; answer comprehension questions.. 268

Grammar builder: Use subject and object pronouns; use comparative adjectives; add "-er" endings to adjectives 270

Let's write: Use question prompts and sentence starters to plan and write a letter; check handwriting and punctuation............................. 272

Chapter 29 274

Speaking and listening: Look at pictures of Jamaican places and take turns to ask and answer questions 274

Word builder: Identify synonyms in context and in a word search 275

Let's read: Read a ghost story and answer questions 277

Grammar builder: Use adjectives in sentences; use adjectives in verbal descriptions................... 279

Let's write: Ask and answer questions about a picture; choose four adjectives which describe the place in the picture; write a description of the place using sentence starters; write a description of another place you know 281

Chapter 30 283

Speaking and listening: Look at pictures, ask and answer questions using the present continuous tense.. 283

Word builder: Use antonyms; change the sound of vowels by adding "r"... 284

Let's read: Ask and answer pre-reading questions; read a text; put pictures of the story in correct sequence; answer comprehension questions.. 286

Grammar builder: Singular and plural possessive pronouns; complete sentences with possessive pronouns; complete sentences with adjectives 288

Let's write: Learn about farming pineapples, and make a mind map of the different activities; draw and write about one of the activities from the mind map; write using question prompts; use adjectives in writing............................. 290

Chapter 31 .... **292**

Speaking and listening: Read aloud the summary of a story; use pictures to retell the story; discuss possible story endings; talk about the role play the story 292

Word builder: Identify and use synonyms and antonyms 294

Let's read: Read a story; ask and answer questions; use and complete a story flow chart, retell the story in your own words 296

Grammar builder: Use adjectives to complete sentences 299

Let's write: Work in groups, use a story flow chart to plan and write a fantasy story 300

Chapter 32 .... **301**

Speaking and listening: Take turns to read aloud a weather report/forecast; look at a weather chart and talk about the symbols and numbers; listen to the weather report again and answer *true* or *false* questions.............................. 301

Word builder: Spell words with "-ble", "-le" and "-dle" ending; find weather vocabulary in a word search 303

Let's read: Read a weather forecast and answer questions 305

Grammar builder: Complete sentences by adding present tense verbs; use "and" to join two related nouns..................................... 306

Let's write: Research your local weather forecast and draw today's weather; write three questions to ask about the weather; write a description of today's weather, using weather vocabulary 308

Chapter 33... **310**

Speaking and listening: Read and role play a conversation with a partner; take turns to ask and answer questions 310

Word builder: Say sight words using picture cues; unscramble letters to form words 312

Let's read: Read a diary entry and answer questions.. 313

Grammar builder: Complete sentences with correct possessive pronouns; rewrite sentences using possessive pronouns; write sentences of your own using possessive pronouns 315

Let's write: Discuss the format of a diary page and talk about keeping diaries; write a diary entry for today............................... 317

Term 3 Unit 1 Review and assessment 318

TERM 1

Unit 1

This term will include playing games, learning about calendars, completing a story and creating a presentation.

Chapter 1

 **Speaking and listening**

1. Work with a partner.
   - Greet your partner.
   - Introduce yourself and ask your partner their name.
   - Ask your partner how they are.

2. Walk around the room. Ask two or three students their name and how they are.

3. Listen to your teacher reading the rules of the game *Rock, Paper, Scissors*.
   1. You need two people. Face your partner and say: "1, 2, 3, Go!"
   2. Make a sign with your hand either of a rock, a sheet of paper or a pair of scissors.

   - To make a rock sign, curl your hand into a fist. A rock can smash scissors, so a rock wins over scissors.

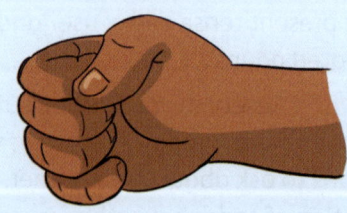

10

- To make a paper sign, hold your hand flat. Paper can cover a rock, so paper wins over a rock.

- To make a scissors sign, hold your index finger (2nd finger) and 3rd finger apart. Scissors can cut paper, so scissors win over paper.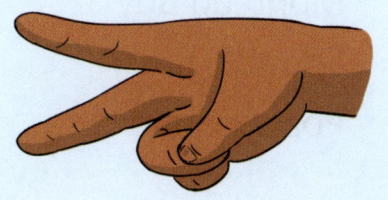

4   Play the game three times. Whoever wins gets a point. The winner is the person with the most points.

Remember ☆☆☆
- Speak clearly.
- Look at your partner when you speak.
- Listen carefully.

5   Your teacher will tell you and your partner whether to use Jamaican Creole (JC) or Standard Jamaican English (SJE) for the following task.
  1   Use Jamaican Creole (JC) to ask and answer questions about the rules. In pairs take turns to interview each other on how to play the game.
  2   Use Standard Jamaican English (SJE) to ask and answer questions about the rules. In pairs take turns to interview each other on how to play the game.

Term 1 Unit 1

Word builder

1. Work in pairs. Put the names of the cities in alphabetical order.

Word box

Kingston	Ocho Rios	Savanna-la-Mar
Montego Bay	Negril	Old Harbour
Spanish Town	Hays	
Port Antonio	Linstead	

_____

_____

_____

2. Listen as teacher reads the poem. Choose a sound that is repeated. Name the letter that makes the sound and write the words in the poem with this sound.

Teddy bear, teddy bear,
Turn around!
Teddy bear, teddy bear,
Touch the ground!
Teddy bear, teddy bear,
Jump up high!
Teddy bear, teddy bear,
Touch the sky!

Teddy bear, teddy bear,
Bend down low!
Teddy bear, teddy bear,
Touch your toe!
Teddy bear, teddy bear,
Turn out the light!
Teddy bear, teddy bear,
Say "good night".

3 Some sounds are made by using both lips together. With your partner, take turns to read these words out loud and notice how you use both lips to pronounce the letters in bold:

- *b* as in **bear** and ca**b**
- *p* as in **p**urse and ra**p**

Put the words under the correct sound – *b* or *p*.

Word box

pig	about	tip	camp
bag	asleep	between	table
lamp	verb	club	pony
be	pan	pot	top
up	before	able	Bob

b	p

Term 1 Unit 1

Let's read

Hello, I am Calvin. This is a picture of me on my bike. I am seven years old. I come from Kingston. There are five people in my family. My favourite subject at school is English. English is fun. My best friend is Michael. He is seven years old. He is in my class at school. My favourite sport is football. I am good at football. My favourite food is goat curry.

1 Complete the sentences.

1 Calvin is _____ years old.

2 He is from _____.

3 His favourite subject is _____.

4 He is good at _____.

2 Circle the correct pronoun to finish each sentence.

1 Calvin has five people in he / his family.

2 Calvin's friend Michael is in her / his class at school.

3 Calvin likes football and he / his is good at it.

4 His / her favourite food is goat curry.

14

3 Complete the family tree with the words in the word box. Then check your answers with your partner.

Word box

brother   ~~Mom~~   sister   Dad

Mom

_____

Calvin

_____

_____

Grammar builder

L👀k and learn

Present tense form of the verb **to be**:

I **am**
You (singular) **are**
He/She/It **is**
We **are**
You (plural) **are**
They **are**

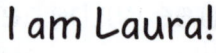

I am Laura!

1 Circle the correct answer.

1 Ben (is)/ are Jamaican.   2 We is / are British.
3 I am / is Donna.   4 It are / is my dog.
5 They am / are my friends.   6 He is / are good at Maths.

2 Complete the text with the words from the word box.

Word box

are   is   are   am   am   is   are

Hi. My name is Emma. I ¹_____ six years old. There ²_____ four people in my family. My sister ³_____ ten years old. We ⁴_____ students at St Catherine's school. My best friends at school ⁵_____ Jackie and Ally. I ⁶_____ good at Art. My favourite sport ⁷_____ basketball.

16

Chapter 1

Let's write

1 Write about you. Use the questions to help you.

> **Remember** ☆ ☆ ☆
> - Check your spelling and punctuation.
> - Check your grammar.

- What is your name?

  My name is _____.

- Where are you from?

  I am from _____.

- How old are you? _____

- How many people are there in your family?

  _____

- Who is your friend? _____

- What is your favourite subject? _____

- What is your favourite day at school? _____

- Who is your Maths teacher? _____

- How many students are in your class? _____

- What is your favourite sport? _____

Chapter 2

Speaking and listening

1 Work with a partner. Take turns to ask each other the questions.

Remember ☆☆☆
- Speak clearly.
- Wait for your partner to finish before speaking.
- Listen carefully.

Example:

I was so happy when I went to the beach with my family. **First**, we packed a picnic for lunch. **Then**, Dad took us to the beach by car. **Next**, we arrived at the beach and found a place to sit. **Last**, we all went swimming. It was a great day!

1 Tell me about a time you were happy.
Where were you? Who was with you?

2 Tell me about a time you were unhappy.
Where were you? Who was with you?

2. Do a class survey. Ask two students the questions in the table and write words or short notes.

	When were you happy?	When were you unhappy?
Name: Delroy	birthday	broke my leg
Name:		
Name:		
Name:		

3. Report back to the class.

> **Example:**
> Delroy was **happy** when it was his birthday.
> He was **unhappy** when he broke his leg.

Term 1 Unit 1

Word builder

1. Write the names of some students in your class in alphabetical order.

> **Remember** ☆☆☆
>
> When you have more than one name that starts with the same letter, you use the second or third letter to write them in alphabetical order. For example: *Aaron, Aidan, Alex, Anthony.*

A a r o n		

Chapter 2

2 Draw a line to match the words to the picture with the same ending sound.

1 box
2 hot
3 cat
4 frog
5 jug
6 tree

3 Work with a partner.
Student A: Say the alphabet silently to yourself.
Student B: After a few seconds, shout "Stop!"
Student A: Call out the letter you were saying, for example: *L*.
Student B: Say a name beginning with that letter, for example: *Lloyd*.

Term 1 Unit 1

Let's read

L👀k and learn

When words end with the same sound, they **rhyme**, for example: *cat / mat*. Poets use rhyme to make their poems interesting and to help you remember them.

This is my friend
Her name is Brie
Brie is kind, and clever
and strong
Her black hair is long
Her eyes are green
Her clothes are always clean
She is good at sports
Brie is good at climbing trees
Brie can climb high like a cat
She can also hit a ball with a bat
She is the best cricket player in my school
On Saturdays, Brie and I go to the swimming pool
Brie can swim fast
She never comes last!

1   Choose two sets of rhyming words from the poem. For each set, draw pictures showing the words. Ask your partner to guess the sets of rhyming words you chose.

    Rhyming Set 1

    Rhyming Set 2

2   Answer the questions.

    1   What does Brie like to climb? _____

    2   What word from the poem rhymes with *peas*?

        _____

    3   What is Brie good at? _____

    4   What do the friends like to do on Saturdays?

        _____

    5   What word from the poem rhymes with *shorts*?

        _____

Grammar builder

> **Look and learn**
>
> A **personal pronoun** is a word that we can use instead of a noun. We can use personal pronouns to replace people and things.
>
> | | Personal pronouns |
> |---|---|
> | **People** | I, you, he, she, we, they / me, him, her, us, them |
> | **Things** | they, them, it |

1 Replace the words in brackets with the correct personal pronouns.

1 Her name is Alice. (Alice) _____ is seven years old.

2 This is my friend Sarah. (Sarah) _____ is in my class.

3 Dan is my brother. (Dan) _____ is a fireman.

4 Calvin likes running. (Calvin) _____ can run fast.

5 Alex and Amy are in my school. (Alex and Amy) _____ live in Kingston.

6 This is my dog Patch. (Patch) _____ is four years old.

7 Alicia is the girl in the red dress. Can you see _____ (Alicia)?

8 The books are on the table. Can you bring (the books) _____ here please?

2 Work with your partner.
  1 Write your partner's name in the gaps of the poem.
  2 Read the poem to your partner.
  3 Now replace your partner's name with the correct personal pronoun and read the poem to your partner again.

I like _____ and _____ likes me.

Being with _____ is my favourite place to be!

Let's write

1 Draw a picture of a friend doing their favourite activity.

2 Think about your friend. Use the questions to help you. Write words from the word box and your own ideas in the spaces.

Word box

black	pretty	short	bike
brown	nice	long	music
green	clever	clothes	TV
funny	strong	sports	food
kind	tall	school	

Chapter 2

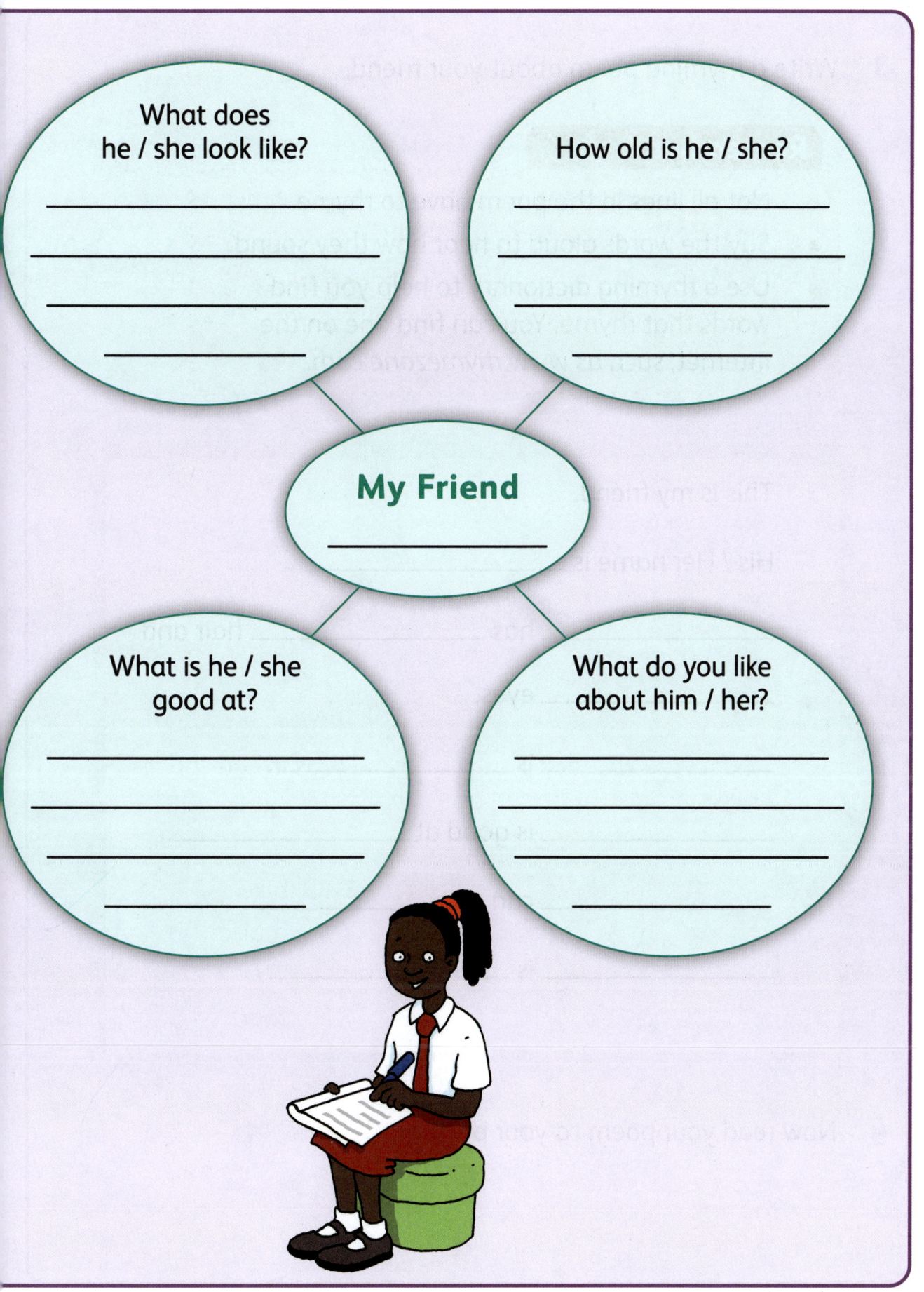

3 Write a rhyming poem about your friend.

> **Remember** ☆ ☆ ☆
> - Not all lines in the poem have to rhyme.
> - Say the words aloud to hear how they sound.
> - Use a rhyming dictionary to help you find words that rhyme. You can find one on the internet, such as www.rhymezone.com.

This is my friend.

His / Her name is _____.

_____ has _____ hair and _____ eyes.

_____ is _____.

_____ is good at _____.

_____ can _____.

_____ is _____.

4 Now read your poem to your partner.

Chapter 3

Speaking and listening

1. With your partner, tell the story using the pictures to guide you. Use the words in the word box and an example for the first picture.

Word box

first   then   next   last

Example:

First, the mother comes into the room. She is very angry because there are toys all over the floor.

Term 1 Unit 1

2 Work with your partner. Add two more pictures to the story.

3 Tell your story and listen to others telling their story.
- With your partner tell your story to another pair of students.
- Ask the students to ask you two questions about your story.
- Now swap and listen to the other students' stories.
- Ask them two questions about their stories.

Word builder

1 Can you remember the alphabet? Tell your partner.

2 Write the names of ten towns, parishes or countries in alphabetical order. For example: *Australia, Barbados*...

_____

_____

_____

_____

_____

L👀k and learn

The vowels **a**, **e**, **i**, **o**, **u** in the alphabet are called **long vowel** sounds.

When **a**, **e**, **i**, **o**, **u** are used in words, they are called **short vowel** sounds.

For example, **a** is usually pronounced *a*, as in *hat*.

3 Write the missing vowel sound for each word.
   Under it, write two more words that rhyme.

1   r___t   2   m___t

3   c___n   4   h___t

5   st___p   6   c___p

7   b___t   8   s___t

4 Look at the words in Activity 3 again. Can you think of anymore rhyming words for the pictures? Say them with your partner.

Example:
rat, cat
mat, fat

Let's read

Last summer, Mary was in London for her holidays. She was with her family. There were four of them, Mary, her sister and her parents. It was the first time she had been in an aeroplane. She was scared at first, but after a while she felt a lot better.

Her aunt lives in London. On the first day she arrived, there was a big dinner. The weather was warm and sunny.

There are lots of fun things to see in London. Mary's favourite place was the British Museum. There were many things to learn there and lots of activities for kids. After two weeks, the holiday was over. Mary was sad because London was really fun.

1 Read the text. Then complete the sentences.

  1 Mary was in _____ for her holidays.

  2 She was with her _____.

  3 Mary's _____ lives in London.

  4 On the first day of their holiday the weather was _____ and _____.

2 Read the text again and answer the questions.
  1 Does Mary often travel by aeroplane?
  2 What was Mary's favourite place in London?
  3 Why did she like it?
  4 How long was Mary on holiday?

3 Close your book and tell your partner about Mary's holiday.

Grammar builder

Look and learn

The past tense of the verb **to be** in the third person.
Lucy **was** at school yesterday.
Dennis **was** in London last year.
He **was not** at work this morning.
It **was** in the tree.

1 The sentences are in the present tense.
Write them in the past tense.

1 My brother is not in Kingston.
_____

2 Tom is a student at St Paul's school.
_____

3 Helen is a teacher.
_____

4 The cat is not in the garden.
_____

5 Rosie is at my house.
_____

2 Write two sentences about yourself in the past.
_____
_____

Let's write

1 Ask your partner about their last holiday. Make notes. Use the questions below.

- Where were you?
- Who were you with?
- What activities were there?
- What was your favourite activity? Why?
- How long were you there?

L👀k and learn

A **paragraph** is a group of sentences about the same idea.

2 Draw a picture of the holiday your partner described.

3 Now write a paragraph about your friend's holiday.

Remember ☆☆☆

- Use the past tense of the verb *to be*.
- Use the correct personal pronouns (*he / she / it / they / him / her / them*).
- When you finish, check for mistakes.

Chapter 4

Speaking and listening

1. Do you know the days of the week? Tell your partner.

2. Take turns to ask and answer the questions.
   1. How many days are there in a week?
   2. How many days begin with T?
   3. How many days begin with S?
   4. What is your favourite day of the week? Why?
   5. What day was it yesterday? What did you do?

3. Do you know the months of the year? Tell your partner.

4. Take turns to ask and answer the questions.
   1. How many months are there in a year?
   2. How many months begin with M?
   3. How many months end with R?
   4. What is your favourite month? Why?
   5. What fun things did you do last month?

5. When is your birthday? Tell your partner how you usually celebrate it.

6. Talk to your partner. Finish the sentences with your own ideas. For example:

   Last Friday I went to the park with my brother and sister. We played football. We were there for two hours.

   Last Saturday…

   Last Sunday…

Word builder

L👀k and learn

Some words have the **th** sound. There are two types of **th** sound – **voiced** and **voiceless**.

You make the voiced **th** sound by sticking your tongue between your front teeth and blowing air out like this:

Words with the voiced **th**: *this, that, those, these, there, they.*

You make the voiceless **th** sound by placing your tongue on bottom teeth and pushing air through like this.

Words with voiceless **th**: *thank, thin, thought.*

An easy way to know whether a sound is voiced or not is to put your finger on your throat and say the word. As you pronounce the sound, feel the shaking (vibration) of your throat. If you feel a vibration the sound is voiced.

1 Work with a partner. Take turns to say the words and write them in the correct place.

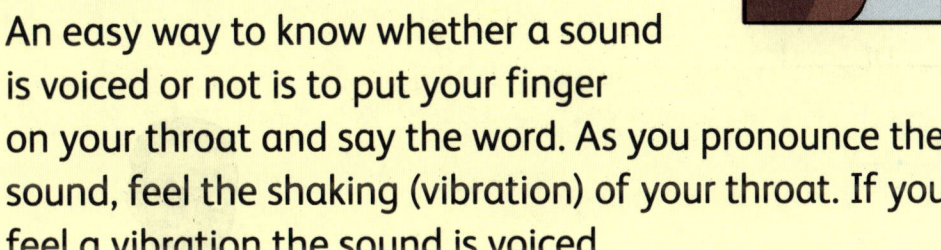

Word box

| than | thumb | think | these |
| then | Thursday | them | thin |

Voiced	Voiceless

2 Add vowels to complete the months of the year.

1 J____nu____ry

2 F____br_____ry

3 M____rch

4 ____pr____l

5 M____y

6 J____n____

7 J____ly

8 _____g____st

9 S____pt____mb____r

10 ____ct____b____r

11 N____v____mb____r

12 D____c____mb____r

Let's read

April 2022

		Wed 13	Thu 14	Fri 15	Sat 16	Sun 17

Mon 18	Tue 19					

1 Look at the calendar. Answer the questions.

1 What do you think is happening from 13th April to 19th April?

2 What will the events be like?

3 What can you do on Friday 15th April?

4 What time can you buy food from Ms Rosie?

5 When can you take part in the talent show?

6 Who can take part in the talent show?

7 When can you see the parade?

Term 1 Unit 1

Grammar builder

L👀k and learn

Just one person
1st person – I or me
2nd person – you
3rd person – he/she
or him/her

SINGULAR

1st person – we or us
2nd person – you
3rd person – they or them
More than one person

PLURAL

Remember ☆☆☆

Pronouns replace nouns in sentences so you do not have to repeat them. Singular third person pronouns are **he, she, it, her, him**.

1 Replace the underlined noun to third person pronouns. Choose from the word box below. Write the pronoun on the line.

Word box

him   her   she   it   she   he

1   <u>Mrs Grace</u> is my English teacher. _____ is a great teacher.

2   <u>The dog</u> is hungry. _____ wants some food.

3   <u>Jack</u> lives on my street. _____ plays basketball with me after school.

4   <u>Liz</u> is a good cook. _____ can make nice cakes.

5   That woman is <u>Peter's</u> mom. I think she looks like _____.

6   Can you give <u>Alice</u> some water please? Can you give _____ some water please?

Chapter 4

Let's write

1   Work with a partner. Make a calendar with some important school dates and holidays.

> **Remember** ☆☆☆
> - Write the months and days in the correct order.
> - Check your spelling.

What you need to make your calendar:

ruler

scissors

coloured card

string

glue

hole punch

41

How to make your calendar.

1. Take a piece of card. Use a ruler to draw seven vertical columns and five horizontal rows.

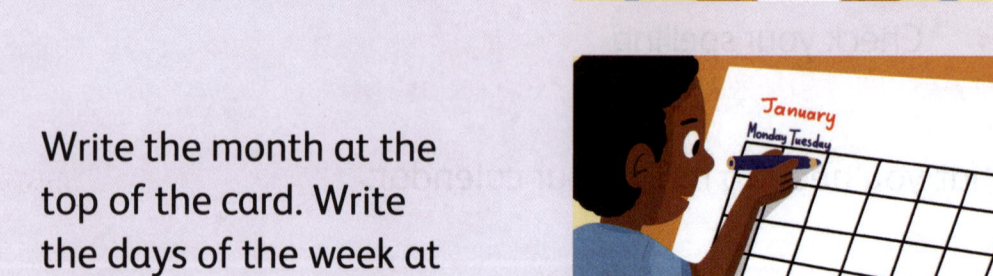

2. Write the month at the top of the card. Write the days of the week at the top of each column.

3. Write the dates.

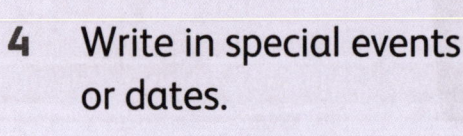

4. Write in special events or dates.

5. Decorate your calendar.

Chapter 5

Speaking and listening

> **Look and learn**
> There are several differences between Jamaican Creole (JC) and Standard Jamaican English (SJE). For example: SJE *things* / JC *tings*.

1 Match the SJE words with the JC words.

1	the		a	fren
2	that		b	elp
3	and		c	an
4	him		d	de
5	help		e	dat
6	friend		f	im

2 Listen to your teacher read or sing the first verse of the song *Mango Time*.

I do not drink coffee, tea – mango time
Do not care how nice it may be – mango time
In the heat of the mango crop
When the fruit all ripe and drop
Wash your pot, turn them down – mango time.

3 Now work with your partner. Take turns to read aloud or sing the first verse of the song in Jamaican Creole.

Mi nuh drink coffee tea – mango time
Care how nice it may be – mango time
In the heat of the mango crop
When di fruit dem a ripe an' drop
Wash yu pot, tun dem dung – mango time.

Term 1 Unit 1

4 Look at the JC words and write the SJE words in the table.

Jamaican Creole (JC)	Standard Jamaican English (SJE)
Mi nuh	
Care how	
… di … dem … an	
… yu … tun dem dung	

5 With your partner, take turns to read out loud or sing the rest of the song in JC. Write out the song in SJE. Check that your SJE version is the same as your partner's.

De terpentine large an fine, mango time
Robin mango so sweet, mango time
Number eleven an hairy skin
Pack di bankra an ram dem in
For di bankra mus' full, mango time.

Mek wi go a mango walk, mango time
For is only di talk, mango time
Mek wi jump pon di big jackass
Ride im dung an no tap a pass
Mek di best a di crop, mango time.

44

Chapter 5

Word builder

1. Draw a line to match the words that rhyme with the pictures.

wet

big

fat

run

sing

clap

2 Colour in the words that rhyme in each set.

1. hat — pin — sat
2. lip — dog — log
3. sun — sip — bun
4. sad — bad — tip
5. hen — bag — pen
6. leg — peg — fell

3 Work with your partner to take turns in reading and spelling.

Student A: Read a word out loud from the first row in Activity 2 while Student B closes their eyes.

Student B: Spell the word.

Student A: Give your partner a point if the spelling is correct.

Swap roles and repeat the above until all rows have been used. The winner is the student with the most points.

Let's read

1. Work with your partner. Look at a picture of a room in a house that belongs to Bedward. A mongoose is entering a room. Describe the picture. What do you think is going to happen?

2. Now read the song. What are the missing words?

Sly Mongoose

Sly Mongoose,

Your name's gone abroad.

Sly Mongoose,

Your name's gone abroad.

Mongoose goes into Bedward's _____ ,

Take out one of them big fat _____ ,

Put him in his waistcoat pocket,

Sly mongoose.

Sly Mongoose

Your name's gone abroad,

Sly Mongoose

Your name's gone abroad.

Mongoose runs into Bedward's _____ ,

There goes one of them big fat _____ ,

Put it in his waistcoat pocket,

Sly mongoose.

3 What do you think the song is about?
Tell your partner.

> **L👀k and learn**
>
> Songs have **patterns** to make them sound good. Some patterns are repetitive. This means that a word or a line in the song is repeated. Some words may have similar sounds such as *kitchen* and *chicken*.

4 Draw a picture to show a part of the poem.

5 Underline the sentences in *Sly Mongoose* that are repeated.

Grammar builder

L👀k and learn

A **plural noun** describes more than one person, place or thing.

For most nouns add **-s**. For example: cat ⟶ cats
For nouns that end in a vowel (a, e, i, o, u) + y (toy) add **-s**.
For example: toy ⟶ toys

For nouns that end in s, z, x, sh, or ch, add **-es**.
For example: church ⟶ churches

For nouns that end in a consonant (b, c, d, f, g…) + o, add **-es**.
For example: mango ⟶ mangoes

1 Write the words in the plural form for these words.

1 toy   _____

2 ball   _____

3 doll   _____

4 book   _____

5 bed   _____

6 pencil   _____

7 pin   _____

8 clock   _____

9 tree _____

10 chair _____

2 Write the plurals of the words in the table. The first one is done for you.

Singular	Plural
glass	glasses
fox	
dress	
church	
wish	
box	
class	
dish	
beach	
toe	
nose	
hero	
mango	

Chapter 5

Let's write

1 Work with your partner. Talk about what makes a good song. Write down three ideas below. For example: *It makes me happy*.

_____

_____

_____

2 Try writing another verse for the song. Complete the gaps with your own ideas.

Mongoose ran into my _____.

He saw a _____ and put it

in his _____.

_____

_____

_____

Remember ☆☆☆

- Make a pattern by repeating some lines.
- Try to think of a few words that rhyme.
- Rhyming words go at the end of a line.
- Read each line aloud to listen to how it sounds.

3 Now sing your song to the class!

Term 1 Unit 1

Chapter 6

Speaking and listening

L👀k and learn

Pictures help you guess what is happening in a story. They can also help you guess what will happen next.

1. Work with your partner. Use the pictures to tell the story about *River Mumma and the Golden Table*.

2. Work with your partner. Use the pictures to tell the story again and this time use the sequence words in the word box.

Word box

First   then   next   lastly

3. Now listen to your teacher tell the story about *River Mumma and the Golden Table*.

Chapter 6

Word builder

1. The words in the table come from the pictures in the story of *River Mumma and the Golden Table*. Work with your partner and find them in the pictures. Write a sentence about what you can see.

bed	The mermaid is on the river bed.
man	The man is looking at the table.
hat	
six	
hut	
pot	

2. Work with your partner and take turns to explain what the words mean in the story.

3. Work with your partner. Say and write any words that rhyme with the words in the table, for example: *bed, head, shed*.

bed _head, shed_____

man _____

hat _____

six _____

hut _____

pot _____

Term 1 Unit 1

Let's read

1 Read the story *Rolling Calf Duppy*.

Mom and her children say goodbye to their friend.

Mom and her children walk home through the forest. The children pick up sticks.

It is dark now and Mom is afraid. Duppies come out at night.

The family arrive at the gatehouse and wave hello to the watchman.

They hear a strange noise. They start to run.

The Rolling Calf Duppy runs after Mom and the children. It is big and scary.

The Duppy sits down and starts counting the sticks.

The watchman was a butcher. Everyone knows when the butcher dies, he comes back as the Rolling Calf Duppy!

2   Look at the story and put the sentences in the correct order. The first, second and third part of the story are written in to help you.

1   Mom and the children say goodbye to their friend. __1__

2   Mom and the children wave at the watchman. __2__

3   The Rolling Calf Duppy runs after the mom and children. __3__

4   The Rolling Calf Duppy counts the sticks. ____

5   The family are at home in their kitchen. ____

6   Mom tells the children to drop their sticks. ____

Check the correct order by looking back at the *Rolling Calf Duppy* story.

3   Draw a line to match the speech bubbles to the people.

"One, two, three…"

"We will get some sticks!"

"He is dead!"

"It is the Rolling Calf Duppy!"

4   Role play the story in groups. One student can be the storyteller, one student can be the mother, one student can be the boy and one student can be the girl.

Grammar builder

Look and learn

The present tense of the verb **to be**:
I **am**
You **are** (singular)
He / She / It **is**
We **are**
You **are** (plural)
They **are**

The past tense of the verb **to be**:
I **was**
You **were**
He / She / It **was**
We **were**
You **were** (plural)
They **were**

1 Write sentences with the present tense of the verb *to be*.

1 Jodie / in / your / class?

   _____

2 John and Bobby / my / friends

   _____

3 you / nine / years old?

   _____

4 the dog / angry

   _____

5 We / from America

   _____

2 Circle the correct answer.
1. The car were / was blue.
2. Yesterday I were / was at my uncle's house.
3. This morning we were / was at school.
4. Where was / were you last night?
5. They was / were at the cinema.

L👀k and learn

To talk about continuous actions that were happening in the past (swimming, playing football or another sport) we use the **past continuous**. This is formed from the past tense of the verb **to be**, together with the **-ing** form of a verb. For example:

Formation of the past continuous tense

past tense of the verb **be** + verb **-ing form**

He **was** read**ing**.

3 Answer the questions using the past continuous. Look at the examples to help you.

1. What were you doing this morning?

   Example:
   I **was** eating breakfast.

2. Ask a classmate what he or she was doing this morning and write what they said.

   Example:
   Alice **was** studying maths.

Let's write

> **L👀k and learn**
>
> A story always has a beginning, a middle and an end.
>
> Stories can be written in the present or past tense. What tense is the *Rolling Calf Duppy* written in?
>
> The **setting** of a story is where and when it takes place. Describing the setting can help make the story more interesting. Where is the setting in the *Rolling Calf Duppy*? What time of day is it?

1. Read the paragraph below and circle the words that tell you where and when the story is set.

> The sun was high in the sky. It was the summer of 2021. Caroline was at the beach with her friends. Caroline was ten years old. It was her birthday and she was very happy.

2. Write a story, starting with this line: *It was almost midnight and Johnny was still awake.*

   - First, draw what happens in the box below.

- Next, use the first sentence and the story planner below to help you write your story.

Beginning: Who is in the story? Where is the setting? What time of day is it?

It was almost midnight and Johnny was still awake.

_____

_____

Middle: What happens?

_____

_____

End: How does it end?

_____

_____

Term 1 Unit 1 Review and assessment

Speaking and listening

1. Work with your partner. Take turns to ask questions.
   Use the prompts to help you make the questions.
   1. How / you?
   2. Where / from?
   3. How old / you?
   4. How many / people / in / your family?
   5. What / favourite subject?
   6. Who / favourite musician or band?

Word builder

1. Circle the word that rhymes with the picture.

1	a hen	b hat
2	a ham	b can
3	a jug	b ten
4	a cat	b pin
5	a gum	b hut
6	a big	b wet

2. Write the words for the pictures in alphabetical order.
   The first two are done for you.

   <u>bat</u>, <u>bug</u>, _____, _____, _____, _____,

61

Term 1 Unit 1

 Let's read

1 Read the text and decide whether the following sentences are true (T) or false (F).

> This summer Kenny was in Wilks Bay with his family. They were in a really nice hotel. It was next to the beach. They were at the beach every day. There were lots of activities at the beach. There were water sports like skiing, surfing and sailing. It was fun! Kenny is good at surfing. He can surf on really big waves. The food at the hotel was delicious. There was Jamaican food and also food from around the world. Kenny's favourite was the Indian food. Near Wilks Bay there was a farm. The family were at the farm one day. There were lots of trees on the farm. There was also a waterfall. Visitors can swim under the waterfall. It is very beautiful.

1 Kenny was in Wilks Bay for his holiday. _____

2 The hotel was on a farm. _____

3 Kenny likes water sports. _____

4 Kenny likes Indian food. _____

5 There is a waterfall on the farm. _____

Review and assessment

1 Complete the table with the correct form of the verb *to be*.

Present tense

I am   We _____

You _____   You are

He / She / It _____ They are

Past tense

I was   We _____

You were   You _____

He / She / It _____ They were

1 Ask a partner about their last holiday and then draw a picture about it. Think about where it was and who was there.

Remember

- Use the correct personal pronouns (*he*, *she*, *it*, *they*, *him*, *her*, *them*).
- Use the past tense of the verb *to be* – *was / were*.

2 Now write a story about your partner's holiday.

_____

_____

_____

_____

_____

_____

_____

_____

_____

Unit 2

Chapter 7

Speaking and listening

L👀k and learn

Taking turns means that one person does or says something, while the other person waits to do or say something. For example, someone listens, while the other person speaks, or plays on a swing, while the other person waits for their turn.

What's your view?
Is it important to take turns? Why or why not?

1. In groups of three role play the conversation below.

Dean: Linda, can I use the computer? Please give me a turn!
Linda: No! I am using it.
Dean: Teacher, Linda will not let me use the computer!
Teacher: Oh, no. You seem unhappy about that. Did you tell Linda how you feel?
Dean: No, I did not.
Teacher: Sometimes it is difficult to wait, but it may help to explain to Linda how you feel.
Dean: Linda, I feel sad that you will not give me a turn.
Linda: OK, Dean, I am nearly done. I will tell you as soon as I have finished.
Dean: Great! Thanks, Linda.

2. Swap roles so you all take turns at role playing the characters (Dean, Linda and the teacher).

3. Tell your group how you felt when you played the role of Dean, Linda or the teacher.

> Example:
> Student as Dean: I felt unhappy when I role played Dean, because it was not fair that I had to wait for my turn.
> Student as Linda: I felt angry, because I was not finished, but after I felt good, because...

4. Play noughts and crosses with your partner.

Takes turns to add either an "O" or a "X" to the board. The first player to line up three of their symbols in a row wins the game. If you need help, ask your teacher.

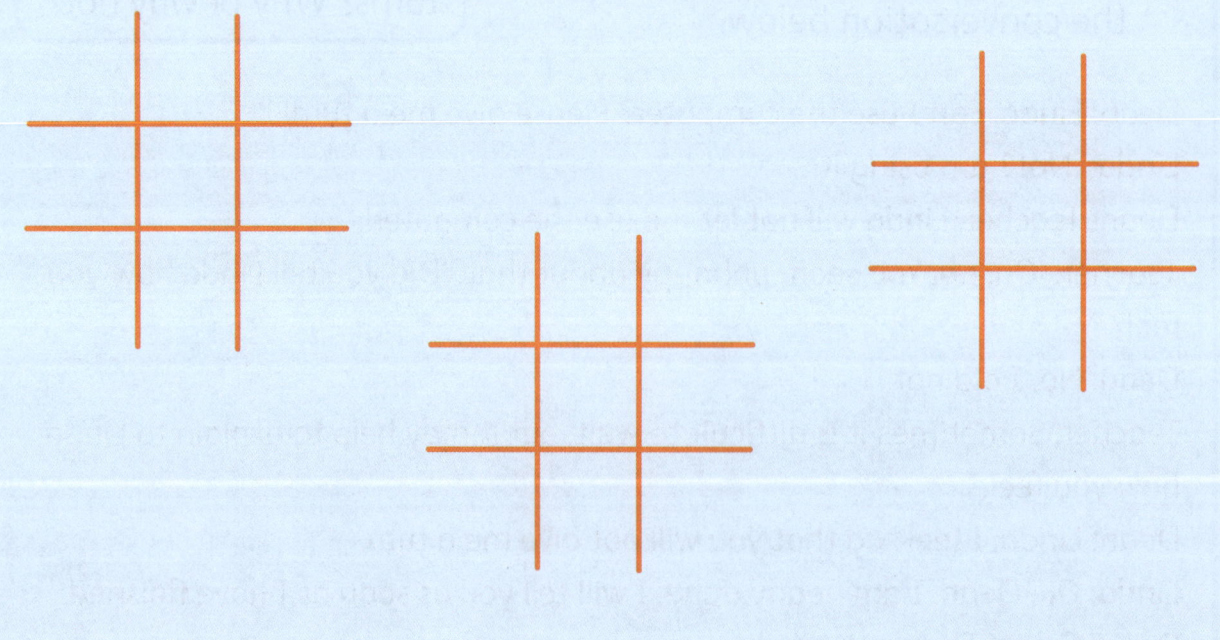

Word builder

Look and learn

When you say the vowels **a, e, i, o, u** as in the alphabet, the sound of the letters is **long**. For example, say the words "ate", "face". The *a* makes the same long sound as saying "A" in the alphabet.

1 With your partner, practise saying the following words with long vowel sounds.

a n**a**me, g**a**me   *i* **i**dea, t**i**me   *u* **u**se, m**u**sic

e h**e**, sh**e**   *o* sn**o**w, **o**ld

2 Look at the words in the circle. They are all about the body. Two of the words have a long vowel sound.

Write them here: _____ _____

> arm   toe
> foot   nose   head
> hand   leg

Look and learn

When we add an **-e** to the end of certain words, it changes the sound and meaning. It makes the vowel sound long, like the way it is pronounced in the alphabet.

3 Read the words and add an -e to make new words.

1 rat_____   2 hat_____   3 pin_____

4 tub_____   5 spit_____

4 Now say the word without the -e (rat) and with the -e (rate). Can you hear the difference?

5 Write the correct words under the pictures.

Word box

| nose | mouth | ears | legs | feet |
| eyes | head | toes | arms | fingers |

_____   _____   _____   _____   _____

_____   _____   _____   _____   _____

Let's read

1. Read the text and correct the spelling mistakes. Write the correct words below.

Our body

What do you see when you look in the mirror? Your body! Our body is made up of lots of different parts. Your fac has eys, a nos, and a muth.

We use our muth to eat food and to make sounds like talking, laughing, crying and singing.

We use our eys to see things. We use our nos to smell. We also have ers. We can hear sounds with our ers.

We have two ams, two hnds and ten fngers. We can use our hnds and fngers to touch and hold things. We have two lgs, two fet and 10 tos. We can walk or run with our lgs and fet.

2 Answer the questions.
1. What is the article about?
2. What parts of the body are on our face?
3. When your friend says something funny, what part of the body do you use to laugh?
4. How do you see things?
5. Which part of the body do we use to smell food?
6. What parts of the body do you use to run?

What's your view?
Do you think that some body parts are more important than others? Share your ideas with your partner.

Chapter 7

Grammar builder

Look and learn

Some past tense verbs are regular. This means we end the verb in **-ed**.

The **-ed** ending in regular verbs in the past tense sounds different. For example, say the word "walked". Does the **-ed** sound like *t*, *d* or *id*? It sounds like *t*.

1 Complete the table with the words from the word box.

Word box

walked	helped	talked	played
carried	skated	washed	chatted
stopped	turned	pointed	watched
called	liked	started	lived

t	d	id
walked		

Look and learn

Punctuation

When do we use a comma? Find examples in the text *Our body*.

Find and circle capital letters in the text. Where in a sentence do we use capital letters?

We also use capital letters for names and places.

Find and underline the full stops in the text. Where in a sentence do we use full stops?

2 Punctuate these sentences correctly and use capital letters where needed.
  1 oranges bananas and pineapples are my favourite fruits
  2 helen is my friend
  3 jack adam and peter are in my class
  4 i can touch things with my fingers
  5 my grandparents live in kingston
  6 london is the capital of britain

Let's write

1. Imagine a monster. Think about these questions:
   - What is its body like?
   - Is it big or small?
   - What colour is it?
   - How many heads does it have?
   - What is its face like?
   - How many arms, hands and fingers does it have?
   - How many legs does it have?

   Draw your monster in the box and write sentences about it.

   _____
   _____
   _____
   _____
   _____
   _____
   _____

Term 1 Unit 2

Chapter 8

 **Speaking and listening**

1. In groups of three, work together to draw a picture and build a story.
   - Student A: On a large blank piece of paper draw a picture of an object using coloured pencils. The object could be a person, an animal, a zoo, a farm, a plant, a school or a house. Now hand the paper to Student B.
   - Student B: Add some details to the picture. Now hand the paper to Student C.
   - Student C: Think about what details you could add to the picture to make it more interesting. Now hand the paper back to Student A.
   - Student A: Should you add more details? Discuss with your group whether the picture needs more details.

2. As a group talk, create the story from the finished picture. You could talk about the part that you added to the picture or agree as a group on the whole story. Use the example sentences to help you.

> **Example:**
> Student A: This is a story about an old house in the forest.
> Student B: Every day, a new plant would grow. After many years…
> Student C: Finally, …

3. Explain how you made the story to the class. Use the group picture to explain your part of the drawing. You need to practise this presentation together and decide who will speak first, second and who will finish the story. Make notes in the organiser.

> **Example presentation starter sentences**
> Student A: I started the picture by drawing a house. I used different colours… Then I gave the picture to…
> Student B: I added some flowers to the garden. I wanted to show that the flowers were very tall and…
> Student C: Finally, …

Introduction	Middle	End
Hello everyone.		
Student A	Student B	Student C

Word builder

> **Look and learn**
> A vowel has two sounds: a long sound, like the alphabet sound *a*, and a short sound as in the word *ant*.

1 Look at the chart below, with examples of when to use a long and a short vowel. With your partner, use a dictionary or online tool to search for other words that have long and short vowels.

Vowel	Long or short	Example word	Your example
a	long *a*	**a**pe, **a**ngel	
	short *a*	**a**nt, **a**pple	
e	long *e*	h**e**, sh**e**	
	short *e*	**e**gg, **e**nter	
i	long *i*	**i**ce, **i**sland	
	short *i*	**i**gloo, **i**tch	
o	long *o*	**o**val, ag**o**	
	short *o*	**o**ctopus, **o**pen	
u	long *u*	**u**nicorn, **u**tensil	
	short *u*	p**u**t, s**u**gar	

76

2 Work with your partner. Colour in and say the words that have long vowel sounds.

hot   note   sad

flute   hike   cup

map   rope   make

dog   cake

sit

Let's read

1 Read the text and circle the words ending in *-ed*. Write some of them below.

_____   _____   _____

2 Circle the correct answer. What tense are the words: present or past?

Hi. I am Angela. Last week I had an accident. I opened the gate outside my house; then, rode my bike to the park. There was a boy in the park; he had a big pole. He used the pole to get something from the lake; it was a kite. When he got his kite, he tried to fly it, but the kite was wet. I said "Goodbye." to the boy and decided to ride my bike to the playground.

I did not see the big hole, so my bike went into the hole and I fell down. I hurt my arm and my head. A woman helped me. She called for help. Then, I went to hospital. I needed a cast on my arm and the doctor also cleaned the wound on my head. It hurt a lot, but I was very brave and I did not cry!

After that, I went home. I was really tired. My mom cooked my favourite food – goat curry with rice and beans. My sister, who is usually very difficult, was kind to me. Then, I watched my favourite TV programme, *The Simpsons*. I like being sick! After that, I went to bed. I was very sleepy.

Chapter 8

> **Remember** ☆☆☆
>
> When an action is in the **past**, we often add **-ed** at the end of the verb or just **-d** if the verb ends with **-e**.
> For example:
> *I walked to school yesterday.*
> *He lived in Kingston when he was a child.*
> We use the **present simple** tense for something that is always true, or something that we do often or all the time.
> For example:
> *I walk to school most days.*
> *He lives near the beach.*

3 Read the text and answer the questions.

1. When did Angela have her accident? _____

2. Where was the accident? _____

3. What body parts did Angela hurt? _____

4 Read the questions. Each has more than one answer. Write two correct answers for each one.

1. Who was at home with Angela?

   _____ _____

2. What did Angela do when she got home from the hospital?

   _____ _____

> **Remember** ☆☆☆
>
> The -e at the end of certain words makes the vowel in the word sound **long**.

79

5 Find words with long vowels from the story that end with a silent *-e*. Write the words below. Take turns to say the words to your partner.

_____

_____

_____

> **Remember** ☆☆☆
>
> Often, you can work out the meaning of a word in a text by the sentences around it.

6 Below are the meanings of some words from the reading text. Write the words next to the correct meanings.

1 something you can ride _____

2 the place you live _____

3 a piece of material that you can fly _____

4 a body of water _____

5 a barrier that you can open and close _____

6 a long piece of wood or metal _____

Grammar builder

1 Complete the sentences with the past tense of the verbs in brackets. Then take turns to say the past tense of the verbs. Decide if the past tense verbs end in the *t*, *d* or *id* sounds.

1 I _____ home from school yesterday. (walk)

2 Peter _____ the ball. (drop)

3 John _____ off the wall. (jump)

4 Nigel and Thomas _____ in the park. (play)

5 The children _____ their homework. (finish)

2 Complete the sentences with the words from the word box in the past tense.

Word box

stop   help   cook   laugh   knock

1 The car _____ me over.

2 I _____ to talk to my friend.

3 My mom _____ my favourite meal.

4 They _____ at my joke.

5 The man _____ me when I fell down.

Term 1 Unit 2

Let's write

1. Write down ideas in the past tense about having an accident. It could be about when you hurt an arm or a leg or someone else had an accident. First, draw what happened.

2. Look at the "Remember" box, use the words below and your ideas from Activity 1 to write your story on the lines below.

Word box

arm	fell	rode	stopped
leg	helped	bike	hurt
head	walked	skated	stitches
hand			

> **Remember** ⭐⭐⭐
> A story has a **beginning**, a **middle** and an **ending**.

Use these questions to help you.
- When and where is the story happening?
- Who was in the story?
- What happened?
- How did it end?

_____

_____

_____

_____

_____

_____

3 When you finish, check your grammar, punctuation and spelling. Then, give your story to a friend to read and check.

Chapter 9

 **Speaking and listening**

> **L👀k and learn**
> **Miming** is a way of acting out something through movement. You do not make sounds when you mime.

1 Imagine you are sick. Choose a word from the box to mime to your partner, but do not tell your partner the word. Your partner has to guess what is wrong. For example, Student A chooses the word "tooth" and mimes a toothache. Student B says "You have a toothache".

head	nose	thumb	tooth
wrist	shoulders	ankle	foot
ear	back	knee	finger
arm	stomach	leg	toe

2 Choose a sentence from the box to mime to your partner, but do not tell your partner the sentence. Your partner has to guess what is wrong and the reason. For example, Student A mimes the sentence about swimming and mimes having sore shoulders. Student B says "You went swimming and now you have sore shoulders".

I went swimming. Now my shoulders hurt.	I carried some heavy boxes. Now I have a backache.
I ate too much ice cream. Now I have a headache.	I have new shoes. Now my foot hurts.
I ate too many sweets and now I have a toothache.	I stepped on some broken glass. Now I have cut my foot.

3 With your partner, write your own sentences that show the reason you are sick ("I went swimming") and the result ("Now I have sore shoulders"). Mime your sentences to another pair of students.

Word builder

1 Circle the pairs of rhyming words in each row.
1. leg   rug   egg   arm
2. feet   meet   head   week
3. sick   wig   kick   pack
4. game   same   home   make
5. face   head   bed   fell
6. bike   gate   make   hike

2 The picture rhymes with the word on the right. Use the pictures to work out the rhyming word and their missing letters. The first one is done for you.

no _se_

by ___

f ___ g

f ___ ll

s ___ nd

Chapter 9

Let's read

L👀k and learn

A **character** is a person in a story. When we describe a character, we often talk about what they are like or how they feel. For example: *He or she is happy, sad, bored, lonely, friendly, kind, cheerful, rude, funny.*

1. Read the text and then ask and answer the questions with your partner.

The day after my accident, my head and my arm hurt a lot. I did not go to school. I stayed at home and watched TV. My mom stayed with me. She cooked my favourite food, goat curry with rice and beans. After a while, TV was boring. I wanted to go outside and play, but my mom said no. I sent my best friend Lucy a text to say hello.

Hey Lucy,
How are you? I am bored.
Come and see me!
Angela x

87

Lucy visited me at home. We played board games; it was fun. I always win at *Monopoly*, but Lucy usually beats me at *Cluedo* as I am not good at working out who did it! Lucy is nine like me. She has a great personality, she is very funny and clever. I am quite shy and quiet. After a while, it was time for Lucy to go home. My teacher, Mrs Jones, gave Lucy some school work for me to do at home until I was better. I was happy because I love school. I am good at English and Maths, but when I tried to write in my notebook I could not hold the pen, so my sister Kelly helped me. We usually fight a lot, but she was really nice to me after my accident! My arm took a long time to heal. It was difficult because I do everything with my right hand and that is the arm I broke. It was also really hot and itchy inside the cast. When the doctor took the cast off, I was really happy. I finally went back to school after four weeks.

1. Who are the characters in the story?
2. How would you describe Angela?
3. How would you describe Kelly?
4. What did Lucy do to help her friend?

2 Complete the table with information about Angela.

Name:	
Age:	
Favourite food:	
Best friend:	
Favourite board game:	
Personality:	
School subjects she is good at:	
How long she stayed at home after her injury:	

Grammar builder

> **Remember**
> We form the past tense by adding **-ed** to regular verbs.

1. Rewrite the sentences in the past tense. Then take turns to read the sentences to your partner.
   1. I walk to school.
   2. James brushes his teeth.
   3. Carly and Vanessa cook dinner.
   4. We watch a movie.
   5. They dance to calypso.

2. Make sentences in the past tense. Use the words in the word box.

   Word box

   plant   jump   miss   paint   play

   1. I / the bus / this / morning
   2. Helen / in / the / pool
   3. Dad / the / house / blue
   4. Jerome / football / in / the / park
   5. We / flowers / in / the / garden

> **Remember** ☆☆☆
> - Use capital letters at the start of sentences, for names and places and when you use "I".
> - Use commas when you list more than two things.
> - Use a full stop at the end of a sentence.

3 Rewrite the sentences below and add capital letters and the correct punctuation.

1. yesterday i was at a party

   _____

2. jackie fell and hurt her leg

   _____

3. peter was sick last week but now he is better

   _____

4. potatoes cucumbers and onions are all vegetables

   _____

5. manchester birmingham leeds and liverpool are cities in england

   _____

6. jerome tripped and fell off his skateboard

   _____

Let's write

1 Write a letter to your friend who is not well and cannot go to school. Answer the questions below to help you write your letter.

Why is your friend sick? *Has a bad cold, hurt their leg…*

What should she or he do at home? *I think you should read, listen to, play…*

Beginning:

Dear Jane,

I know you are not very well. I heard _____

_____

_____

Middle:

If you are bored, you should _____

_____

_____

_____

End:

I hope you get well soon. I will see you _____

_____

_____

Term 1 Unit 2

Chapter 10

Speaking and listening

1. Listen and respond to your partner giving you instructions.

   Example:
   Student A: Draw a square, put a dot in the middle of the square, place an x to the left of the square.

   Is this correct?

   Student B draws the picture based on the instructions and shows picture to Student A to check if it is correct.

2. Work in groups of three or four. Imagine you have a box. This box can look different to different people in your team. First, each person in the team should think about the questions below. Then, ask and answer the questions with your group.
   - What shape is it?
   - What does the box look like? Think about its colour and size.
   - What is the box made of? (wood, cardboard, paper…)

3. Now imagine there is something inside the box. Each person in your group takes the object out, holds it and mimes actions to show what it is. Do not say what the object is! The other students try to guess.

Chapter 10

Word builder

1 Help Harold find his way across the river.
Draw a line to the rhyming words.

2 Say the words. Then complete the word.

1	may	say	d____
2	fed	bed	r____
3	hat	cat	s____
4	cake	lake	m____
5	men	pen	t____
6	jar	car	f____

> **Remember** ☆ ☆ ☆
>
> In Chapter 7 you learned that we make a long vowel sound when we add an **-e** to the end of certain words.
> - The **-e** is silent, for example: *gate*.
> - Sometimes adding an **-e** elongates the vowel sound and makes a new word. This is often called "the magic **-e**" because it changes the sound and meaning of the word. For example: *rat, rate*.

3 Read the word and add the magic *-e* to make a new word. The first one is done for you.

Vowel	Example word	+ magic -e
a	mat	mate
e	pet	
i	hid	
o	not	
u	cub	

Let's read

1. Read the story. Then close your book and take turns to tell your partner what the story was about.

A Game of Charades

Alison is at St Christopher's Primary school. She is ten years old and she loves to play charades. Last week she took part in a school charades competition. She was on a team with three other people, and she was the team leader. Alison was a great team leader. She made sure everyone in the team took part. Her best friend, Charlie, was also on the team. Charlie is very funny, but sometimes a bit lazy.

Alison and her team played against St Thomas' Primary school. On the St Thomas' team, there were four members. One of the members was Ben. Ben lives near Alison, but they do not like each other. Alison thinks Ben is a bully. One day, when Alison was coming home from school, Ben threw a ball at Alison's head and called her nasty names, so Alison was not happy when she saw that Ben was on the other team.

The two teams played an exciting game against each other. Each team got up onto the stage to act out a movie or song and the other team had to guess what it was. Everyone enjoyed watching the game. At the end of the game, St Thomas' team won. Alison and her team were very disappointed. Then, a girl from St Christopher's, said she saw a team member from St Thomas' listening to the other team as they planned what charades to use. Guess who that team member was. Ben! So, the results were changed and St Christopher's players were the winners!

2 Write notes about each of the characters. Think about their personalities and the words in text that describe them. For example: *great, funny, lazy*.

Alison: _____

Charlie: _____

Ben: _____

3 Share your notes with your partner and talk about the characters. Use the questions to help you.

- Which character did you like the most? Why?
- Which character did you like the least? Why?
- Which team did you want to win? Why?

4 Think about a time you played a game with someone, or a competition where you took part in teams. Talk about it with your partner. Use the questions to help you.

- What was the game?
- Who did you play with?
- How did you feel? 😊 😐 ☹
- How would you feel if someone cheated during a game? 😊 😐 ☹

Grammar builder

1. Complete the text with the past tense verbs.

Word box

enjoyed   played   skipped
jumped   tripped   played

I like to play lots of games with my two best friends, Vicky and Robert. Last weekend we ¹_____ *Dandy Shandy*. It was a fun game and I really ²_____ it. When it was my turn to be in the middle, I ³_____ out of the way of the ball. That ball did not hit me once! We also ⁴_____ *Brown Girl in the Ring*. Vicky ⁵_____ while Robert and I swung the rope. When it was Robert's turn, he ⁶_____ and fell. He hurt his leg, but now he is better. Sometimes we also play board games. Robert is very good at *Scrabble*. He can think of lots of different words and he can spell very well.

2 Find and correct the spelling and grammar mistakes in the sentences. Which words in the sentences tell us we are talking about the past?

1. We passd our exams! We got our results today.

   _____

2. The bus arrives late yesterday.

   _____

3. Carol calls me last night.

   _____

4. The dog chasd the cat last Saturday.

   _____

5. Mark cheats on the test this morning,

   _____

6. The baby pickid up the toy.

   _____

Chapter 10

Let's write

1. Prepare to write a report about a real game.

> **L👀k and learn**
> A **report** is a non-fiction text based on what actually happened. A report usually has a title which tells you what it is about.

2. Use the questions below to help you write your report about a game you watched.
   - What was the game?
   - Who were the team members?
   - Who did they play against?
   - Where did the game happen?
   - What did you like about the game?
   - What did you not like?
   - Who won the game?

> **Remember** ☆☆☆
> - Use the past tense.
> - Check your spelling, grammar and punctuation.
> - Give it to your friend to check.

Write your report here:

_____

_____

_____

_____

_____

_____

99

Term 1 Unit 2

Chapter 11

 **Speaking and listening**

1. Take turns to read aloud a paragraph to your partner. Underline any words you do not understand.

2. Ask your partner one question from each paragraph.

Example: "How many gold medals did Usain Bolt win at the Rio Olympics?"

"He won three."

3. With your partner, discuss which headings match the paragraphs.

Early Life

Getting well

An Olympic Champion

1 _____

Usain Bolt is the fastest runner in the world. He won three gold medals at the 2016 Rio Olympics. In total, he has won nine Olympic gold medals for sprinting, but one was taken away because a team member broke the rules.

2 _____

Usain was born on 21 August 1986 in Trelawny, a small town in Jamaica. He lives with his parents, his brother Sadiki and his sister Sherine. When he was young, Usain loved to play cricket and football in the street with his brother. When he started secondary school, his coach Pablo McNeil noticed that young Usain was very fast. After that, Usain took part in competitions.

3 _____

Then, when Usain was in his twenties, doctors told him he had a problem with his back. But Usain wanted to do sports. He did not give up. He had to make his back strong. So, Usain exercised every day and made his back stronger. Usain did not allow his problem to stop him from making his dream come true – to be a great Olympic champion. When it was the 2008 Beijing Olympics, Usain was ready – he won three gold medals! He then went on to win three more gold medals for running in the 2012 Olympics in London.

Term 1 Unit 2

Word builder

L👀k and learn

Context clues are hints you should use to work out missing information or the meaning of unfamiliar words and phrases. What is missing from the picture?

Clues: You already know about what kind of animals like eating bones. You already know what animals stay in a kennel. You know what kind of animals are called Patch. So, the answer is probably *a dog*.

1. Look at the text again about Usain Bolt in the "Speaking and listening" lesson. Use clues in the text to complete the table about Usain Bolt.

Example:

Age: Look at the year he was born in the text (21 August **1986**).
What is the **year** now?
Count the number of years between the years to work out how old he is now.
Ask your teacher to check your answer.

Name:	
Age:	
Sport he is famous for:	
Number of brothers / sisters:	
Favourite childhood games:	
Number of Olympic medals:	
Personality: (circle)	shy quiet strong brave friendly kind happy

2 Work with your partner. Take turns to tell each other about Usain Bolt. Use the information in the table in Activity 1.

Usain Bolt is famous for ¹_____.

He is ² _____ years old. He has

³ _____. His favourite

⁴ _____. He has won

⁵ _____. He is ⁶ _____.

Let's read

1 Read the information in the table with your teacher.

Question-Answer Relationship (QAR)

IN THE TEXT

Right There

The answer is in one place in the text. The words from the question are often repeated in the text.

- Quickly reread and **scan** to find exact information.
- Look for key words.

Think and Search

The answer is found in different parts of the text.

- Quickly reread and **skim** to find general information.
- Look for important information.
- Link different parts of the text to answer the question.

IN MY HEAD

Author and You

The answer is not in the text.

- Think about what you know and what is in the text – how does this link together?
- Reread.
- Predict.

On Your Own

The answer is not in the text.

- Think about your own experience.
- Think about what you have read before.
- Make connections.

2 Look at the text in the "Speaking and listening" lesson and answer the QAR questions. Match the "Right There" questions and answers.

1. Where is Usain Bolt from?

2. How many gold medals did Usain Bolt win at 2016 Olympics?

3. Where was the Olympics games held in 2008?

three

Beijing

Jamaica

3 Answer the "Think and Search" question.

Where were the Olympic games held in:

2008? _____   2012? _____   2016? _____

4 Answer the "Author and You" question.

Do you think that Usain Bolt will win more gold medals in the next Olympic games?

_____

5 Answer the "On Your Own" question.

Think of someone that is as great or nearly as good as Usain Bolt. Who is this person and why do you think they are so talented?

_____

_____

Check your answers with your partner.

Grammar builder

Remember ☆☆☆

Regular verbs in the past
If the verb ends in **-e**, just add **-d**.
For other regular verbs add **-ed**.

Present → Past	Sound of the verb ending:
bake → bake**d**	t
play → play**ed**	d
paint → painte**d**	id

Look at the information below about Usain Bolt.

1. Underline the regular verbs in the past tense. Check your answers with your partner.

2. Take turns with your partner to say out loud the regular past tense verbs. Do the verb endings sound the same or are they different?

> Usain loved to play cricket and football in the street with his brother. When he started secondary school, his coach Pablo McNeil noticed that young Usain was very fast. Usain wanted to do sports.

3 Now write the verbs in the table in the past tense. Sound them out as you write them and put the sound *t*, *d* or *id* next to the verb.

	Yesterday I…	Sound
walk	walked	t
learn		
enjoy		
jump		
pick		
visit		
start		
watch		

4 Write sentences about yourself with the past tense of the verbs.

> **Example:**
> Visit – Last week I **visited** my grandparents.

Let's write

1 Work in groups of three or four. Think about a sports hero you like and prepare to write three paragraphs about him or her.

Before you begin to write, plan your writing:
- Research the sports person on the internet.
- Find out interesting facts about the person.
- Make notes on the information you find.

Name:	
Age:	
Sport he or she is famous for:	
Number of brothers / sisters:	
Favourite childhood games or hobbies:	
Number of Olympic medals:	
Any medals:	
Personality:	

2 Use the questions to help you write the paragraphs.

Paragraph 1

What is his / her name?

Why is he / she famous?

What competitions did he / she win?

Paragraph 2

Where and when was he / she born?

How many brothers / sisters do they have?

What was their childhood like?

When did they start the sport?

Paragraph 3

What problem or challenge did they have in their life?

How did they get over it?

Why do you like the person?

_____
_____
_____
_____
_____
_____
_____
_____
_____
_____
_____
_____
_____
_____
_____

Chapter 12

 **Speaking and listening**

1. Work in groups of three or four. Prepare a presentation for the class about your sports hero. Use the information your group researched in the "Let's write" lesson in Chapter 11.

   - Decide what each team member is going to talk about.
   - Use the internet to find pictures of your sports hero.
   - Use your notes from your "Let's write" lesson in Chapter 11 and the plan below to guide you.

   Use the plan below to help you.

		Notes
Beginning	**Introduce** the person and why they are famous. **Show** some pictures. **Say** what competitions they have won.	
Middle	**Talk about** the person's early life. **Describe** their family and how they started sports.	
End	**Talk about** a difficulty in the person's life and how they got over it. **Conclude** – Remind everyone of the key points in your presentation and ask them if they have any questions.	

Look and learn

When you **summarise** something, you write or say the general idea and the most important points.

Example:

Beginning: The person who is our hero is Usain Bolt. He is famous because he is the fastest runner in the world. Here is a picture of him. He won eight Olympic medals for sprinting. In 2008 he… Now my classmate will talk about…

Middle: Hello everyone, I am Anna. When Usain was young he lived… He went to… He was good at…

End: Hi everyone, finally I will summarise…

Remember

- Speak clearly and loud enough so people at the back of the classroom can hear you.
- If you forget something, look at your notes.

Word builder

1 Work with your partner. Look at the pictures.
What are they? Why do you use them?

2 With your partner, choose three items. Try to spell their names. Compare your spellings with your partner. Who do you think is correct?

_____   _____   _____

3 Work with your partner. Match the words to their meanings.

1 learn   a a website about a topic
2 blog   b something that you work on
3 help   c feeling joy
4 different   d to study something
5 happy   e to make something easier
6 information   f the opposite of the same
7 code   g instructions that tell a
8 project   computer what to do
                  h facts about something

Chapter 12

Let's read

Hi! My name is Emily and I go to St Mary's Primary school in Kingston. Last month my class got our first computers, it was great! We started computer lessons. I was really happy because I want to learn more about computers. They are really fun and they help us do important things.

Mr Radcliffe teaches us about the computer. He is a great teacher. We learned about the different parts of the computer and what they are used for. The best part of the lesson was when we used the internet to find out information. I worked with Lisa – she is my best friend. We found a blog about our favourite singer, Rihanna. We also found some pictures of her and Mr Radcliffe showed us how to print them.

Our next project was to make a computer game. We did this by learning to write a code. We used the computer to draw pictures for the game. We used code to make the characters in the game move. It was lots of fun!

L👀k and learn

We use question words to find out information.

Some question words start with the letters *Wh-*:

What, Who, When, Where, Why.

1 Answer the questions.
   1. Where does Emily go to school?
   2. What did Emily and her class get last month?
   3. Who is Mr Radcliffe?
   4. What does Emily think of computers?

2 Use the text and your own ideas to answer the questions.

   1. Does Emily like Mr Radcliffe? Explain how you know.

   _____
   _____

   2. Do you think Emily likes going to school? Explain why.

   _____
   _____
   _____

   3. What did Emily do on the computer?

   _____
   _____

   4. Do you think you are similar to Emily, or different? Explain why.

   _____
   _____

Chapter 12

Grammar builder

1 Find and write down all the past tense verbs in the "Let's read" lesson.

_____

Use the verbs to write three sentences about yourself.

> **Example:**
> Last week my parents took me to the beach, it **was** a lot of fun.

1 _____

2 _____

3 _____

Compare your sentences with your partner and check each other's work for neat handwriting and correct punctuation.

2 Look at the pictures and complete the sentences with the correct past tense verb.

> **L👀k and learn**
> We use *time expressions* to talk about events in the past. For example: *last week*.
> What time expressions for the past do you know?
> Can you find a past time expression in the text about Emily in the "Let's read" lesson?

115

1 Yesterday, I _____ (speak) to Julie on the phone.

2 Last weekend, we _____ (play) computer games.

3 Last summer break, all my classmates _____ (email) each other.

4 This morning, I _____ (talk) to my aunt on Skype. She lives in London.

What is the irregular past tense verb in Activity 2?

_____

How do you know it is not a past tense regular verb?

_____

L👀k and learn

Verbs are **regular** or **irregular**.
Regular verbs: *bake / baked*
Irregular verbs: *write / wrote*.

Let's write

1 Think about a community event or school project when you and your friends used computers. Write a story about it. Use the questions and time expressions to help you.

Word box

yesterday
last week / month / year
two / three days ago
last night

- When did the event happen?
- Where did it happen?
- Who were you with?
- What did you do?
- What did you learn?
- Did you enjoy the event? Why? Why not?

_____

_____

_____

_____

_____

Term 1 Unit 2 Review and assessment

Speaking and listening

1. Work with your partner. Look at the picture and use the words to label and say the parts of the body.

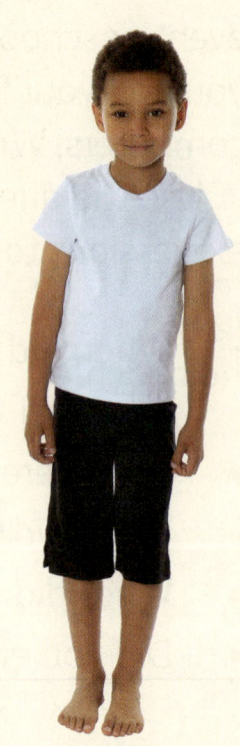

Word box

legs	arms	nose	hair
head	feet	ears	
face	fingers	mouth	
toes	eyes	body	

Word builder

1. Match the words to the pictures that rhyme. Then say the words.

race   same   cone   mice   hate   jar

Let's read

After school on Friday, David was at a birthday party. All the boys and girls were dancing to music at the party. David also wanted to dance. So, he decided to breakdance. At first, he was great! Everyone made a ring around David while he danced. Then, suddenly David fell down. He hurt his arm and his leg. It hurt a lot, so his friends called his parents. They called an ambulance and went to the hospital.

When David arrived at the hospital, the doctor came to look at him. The cut on his leg was quite big and he needed stitches. The doctor x-rayed his arm and saw that it was not broken. He gave him some medicine for the pain and David felt better.

When David got home, he felt really tired, so he went to bed early. The next day, he felt a bit better, but his arm and leg hurt. It was a nice sunny day and his parents decided to go to the beach. He wanted to swim in the sea, but his parents said "no", so he started to build a sandcastle with his baby sister. After two weeks, his arm and leg were much better, and he was able to play basketball again!

1 Read the text. Circle the correct answer.

1 Where did David have his accident?

a  b

2 What body parts did David hurt?

 a 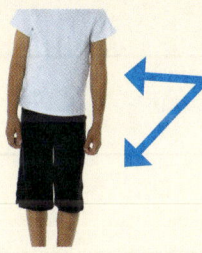 b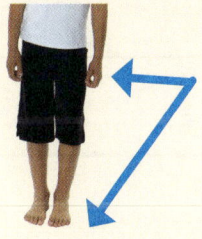

3 How did he go to the hospital?

 a 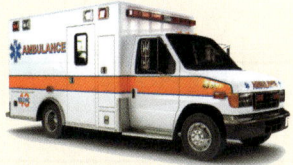 b

4   What body parts did the doctor x-ray?

a      b

5   What did David do at the beach?

a      b

1   Write a story about being sick or injured.
    Use the past tense and the questions below to help you.
    • Who are the characters in the story?
    • Where does the story take place?
    • When does the story take place?
    • What events happen?
    • How does the story end?

    _____
    _____
    _____
    _____
    _____

Unit 1

This term will include playing games, learning about calendars, completing a story and creating a presentation.

Chapter 13

Speaking and listening

Pre-listening questions
- How do you feel when you first dip your feet into the sea or a swimming pool?
- What does it feel like when the sun is hot and you cannot look at the sky?

1. Work with your partner. Take turns to say the poem. When your partner speaks, close your eyes and imagine the scene.

The Sea and the Sun

The sea tastes like ice
The sea smells like the wind blowing
The sea sounds like someone clapping
The sea feels like wet clouds
The sea looks like glass.

The sun smells like bread
The sun sounds like a hurricane
The sun tastes like sugar cane
The sun feels like fire
The sun looks like gold.

2. Tell your partner how each line of the poem makes you feel.

Talk about the difference between the first part of the poem and the second part, and how it makes you feel.

> **Example:**
> The sea tastes like ice; it makes me feel cold and reminds me of ice floating in water.

3. Imagine you are eating an orange. Think about how it smells, feels, looks, tastes and sounds when you eat it. Take turns to describe this to your partner.

4. Think of a time you ate with other people. For example, if you had a picnic at the beach or a meal at a restaurant. Answer the questions, then tell your partner what it was like.

- Who was there?

   I had a picnic with my friend...

- Where did you eat?
- What did you eat?
- What was it like?

Chapter 13

Word builder

Look and learn
Consonants that blend:
- Some consonants blend together, but you can still hear each sound. For example: **cl**oud, **bl**ack (look at Activity 1).
- Some consonants blend together, but only make one sound. For example: **th**umb, **ch**eese (look at Activity 2).

1 Look at the pictures:
- Say the consonant blend at the start of the word: *cl, br, cr, cr, br, bl*. Can you hear each sound?
- Now say the rest of the word: *clock, brown, crab, crayon, broom, blue*.
- Find and circle the words in the word search. The word *crayon* is done for you.

clock

brick

crab

p	w	w	w	c	r	a	y	o	n
z	q	s	g	s	o	p	t	r	c
j	k	v	x	c	r	a	b	h	c
f	w	g	b	o	b	t	r	j	h
b	r	i	c	k	l	n	p	b	o
p	a	q	i	c	u	h	d	d	d
v	e	i	f	l	e	c	l	n	n
q	c	b	r	o	o	m	s	u	b
y	u	a	i	c	e	r	q	m	e
l	s	y	v	k	m	l	a	v	w

crayon

broom

123

Term 2 Unit 1

2 Complete the words with the correct letters from the word box.

Word box

ch   sh   th   wh   ch   th

1 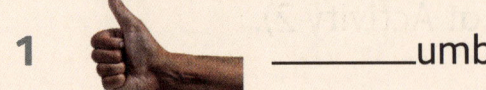 _____umb

2  ba_____

3  _____eese

4  _____oe

5  _____ild

6  _____ale

Chapter 13

Let's read

L👀k and learn
A **simile** is a way of describing something by comparing it to something else. To do this we use **like** or **as**. For example: *She is **as** light **as** a feather.*

1. Look at the poem *The Sea and Sun* in the "Speaking and listening" lesson. With your partner, talk about the similes and why you think the two things are compared.

Example:  Why does the poem say "The sea tastes like ice"?

 Maybe because the sea is cold and it reminds the writer of ice.

2. Read the poem *The Forest* and draw a picture about the poem.

125

The Forest

The forest smells heavy like the air before rain
The forest tastes like the colour green
The forest sounds like the crunching of leaves
The forest looks like a magic kingdom
The forest feels as soft as a baby.

The forest smells like the Earth
The forest tastes like the colour brown
The forest sounds like the songs of birds
The forest looks like wet tears
The forest feels as quiet as the night.

What's your view?
How is the poem *The Sun and the Sea* similar to *The Forest*?

3. Choose three similes from the poem and explain to your partner why you think they are compared.

Example:
The forest smells heavy like the air before rain.

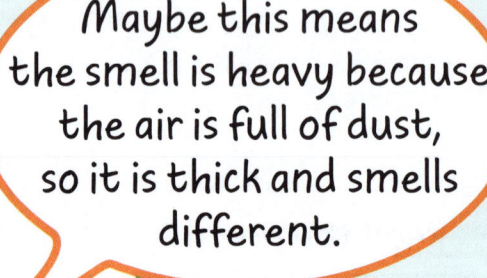

Maybe this means the smell is heavy because the air is full of dust, so it is thick and smells different.

4. Now choose something about you (your smile, your legs, your hair) and write a simile about yourself. For example: *My eyes are like brown stones, My hair is like a lion's mane.* Compare your simile with your partner.

Grammar builder

> **Look and learn**
> To make questions, we often use the verbs **to do**, **to have** and **to be**. For example:
> like / mangoes?   *Do you like mangoes?*
> have / a bag?   *Do you have a bag?*
> this / your book?   *Is this your book?*

1 Reorder the words to make questions.

1 you / eat / rice / do?
   _____

2 this / your / bag / is?
   _____

3 he / have / does / pet / a?
   _____

4 Lucy / does / in / Kingston / live?
   _____

5 is / that / sister / your?
   _____

6 you / like / English / do?
   _____

2 Match the questions to the answers.

1 Do you watch SpongeBob?
2 Is this your crayon?
3 Does she have a sister?
4 Does he play football?
5 Do you have a pencil I can borrow?

a Yes, he does.
b No, it is not.
c Yes, I do.
d Yes, she does.
e Yes, I do.

3 Complete the questions with the correct words.

Word box
Does / have   Is   Do   Do / like

1 _____ you _____ bananas? — No, I do not.

2 _____ this your pen? — Yes, it is.

3 _____ Grace _____ a mobile phone? — Yes, she does.

4 _____ you play tennis? — Yes, I do.

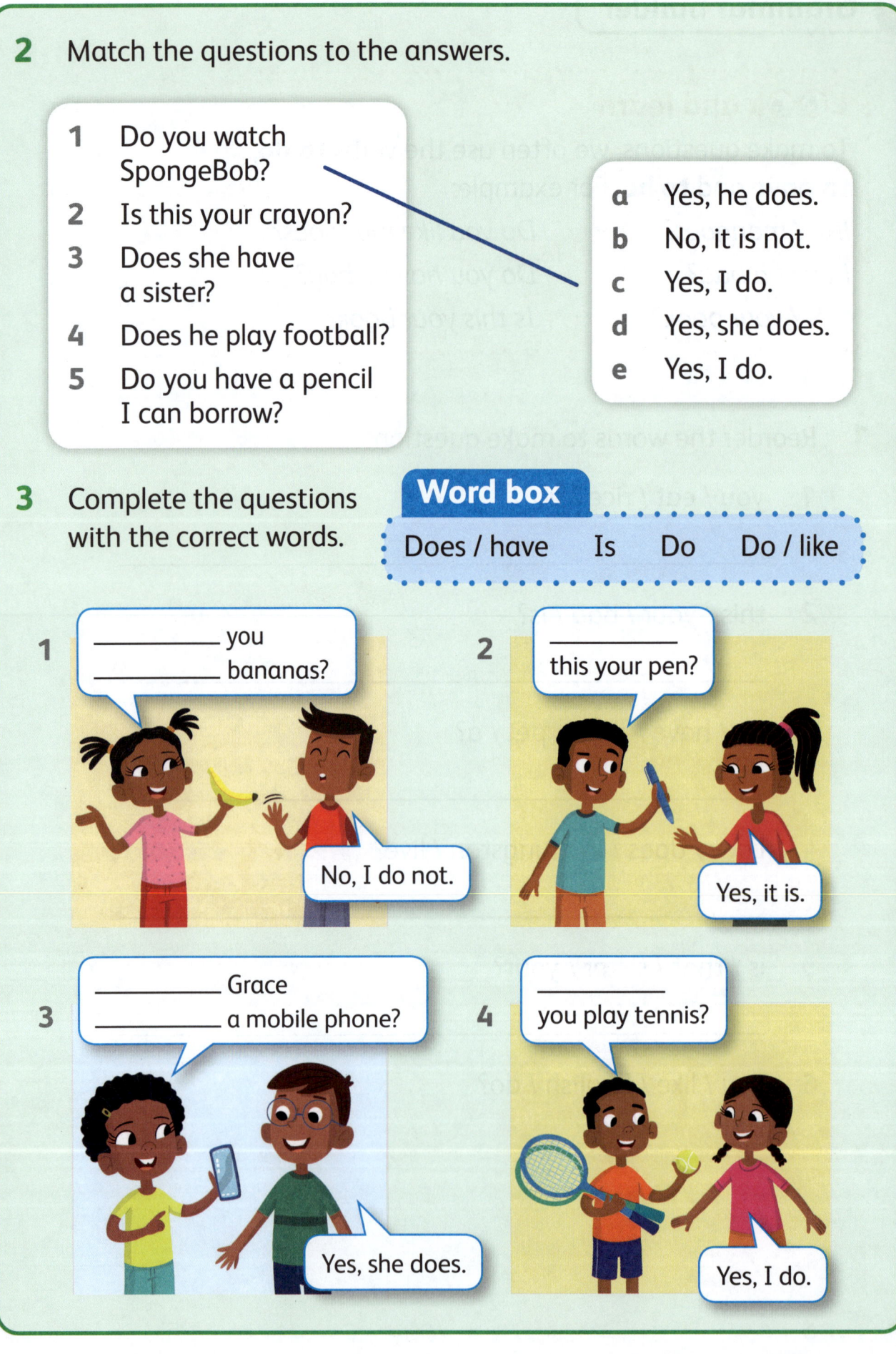

Let's write

1. Work in groups of two or three. You are going to write a short poem. Choose a topic to write about from the titles below.

   the sea   the sun   the mountains

   rivers   waterfalls   rain

2. Use your feelings, senses and similes to describe your group's ideas for the poem. Write answers to the questions to help you with ideas.

   What does it sound like? _____

   What does it taste like? _____

   What does it feel like? _____

   What does it look like? _____

   What does it smell like? _____

Remember ☆☆☆

When you use **similes**, you use your imagination and even write about things that do not make sense. For example: *The forest feels as soft as a baby.*

3 Now write your poem.

_____ sounds like _____.

_____ tastes like _____.

_____ feels like _____.

_____ looks like _____.

_____ smells like _____.

4 When you finish, read your poem to the class.

Chapter 14

Speaking and listening

1. Work with your partner. Use the phrases below the pictures to role play the conversations.

> ### L👀k and learn
> **Body language** shows how people really feel through the look of their face and their body movements. This is important when you speak in public. For example, if you need to give a presentation to your class you need to:
> - look at your classmates' faces
> - smile and look happy
> - hold your head up high
> - do not play with your hands or your hair
> - stand up straight.

Pre-listening questions
- Have you ever had to speak to a lot of people together? Perhaps you had to say thank you for your presents at your birthday party or tell a story to people you do not know very well.
- How did you feel? Were you happy, scared, confident?

2 Your teacher will read the following text to you.

Before your teacher starts, discuss with your partner what you think the text is about.

Here is why the way we look and move is so important:

> People try to look confident, but their body language may show that they are unsure about themselves. They may say "I am really happy and excited to be here.", but their face, head, shoulders, hands and all of their body may show that they are not happy.
>
> If you are giving a presentation to your class, you may say "Hello everyone, I am really pleased to talk to you today about…", but without knowing it, your body language shows the opposite. At the end of the presentation, you may feel you did really well, but maybe the audience, your classmates, thought you were scared, bored, unhappy or angry, because your head was on one side, your face showed you were bored, your shoulders were forward and your hands were shaking.
>
> So, we may not say something out loud, but our body language will let everyone know how we really feel.

3 Discuss what parts of the body were mentioned in the text. Make a list of the body parts here.

_____

_____

4 With your partner, talk about what you think the phrases mean and make notes below. Do not worry if you do not know the exact meaning of each word, just use the words as clues to guess the meaning of the phrases. The first one is done for you.

Body language includes:

1 eye contact

<u>To look at someone's face.</u>

2 facial expressions

_____

3 head movements

_____

4 hand gestures

_____

5 body posture

_____

5 Check your meaning of the phrases with another pair of students.

Report back to the class and compare your understanding of the phrases with your classmates.

Term 2 Unit 1

Word builder

Remember ☆☆☆

Consonants that blend:
- Some consonants blend together, but you can still hear each sound. For example: **bl**ock, **cl**ap.
- Some consonants blend together, but only make one sound. They are made with the letters *ch, sh, ph, th, wh, kn, wr*… For example: **ch**air, **sh**ell.

1 Circle the correct consonant blend to complete the word. Then write each sound.

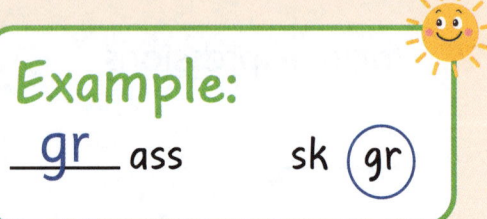

Example:

__gr__ ass   sk (gr)

1 _____ove   bl   gl

2 _____ock   cl   gr

3 _____ick   br   bl

4 _____um   tr   dr

2 Draw lines to match the consonant blend to the rest of the word.

1 ch   oto

2 ph   umb

3 sh   alk

4 th   eep

134

3 Colour the pictures that have the same consonant blends with the same colour. Write the consonant blend in the box.

Let's read

1 Look at the pictures around paragraph A. What do you think the text will be about? Now read the text. Were your predictions right or wrong?

A
I skated to school yesterday
On the way, I saw my cousin May
Then I turned to cross the road
And a car came and knocked me down
They took me to the hospital in town
They dressed me in a hospital gown.

2 Look at the picture next to paragraph B. What do you think the text will be about? Now read the text. Were your predictions right or wrong?

B
The car hit my leg
It broke like an egg
I was in lots of pain
So I cried like the rain
Then the doctor came in
He told me with a grin
That a cast would fix my bone
So that I could go home.

Remember ☆☆☆
- Every partner should give their ideas.
- Listen when your partner speaks.

3 Read the final paragraph of the poem below with your partner. Decide which words from the word box should go in each space and write them in. Then take turns to say the poem to each other.

Word box

cast   fast   me   at last

> My friends came to visit _____
>
> They wrote their names on my _____
>
> I was happy to see them.
>
> But their visit was so _____
>
> The next day I smiled.
>
> I was going home _____!

4 With your partner, look at the poem again. How many pairs of rhyming words can you find?

5 Talk about whether you liked the poem or not.

Example:

I liked the poem, because it shows how you must be careful on the road.

Term 2 Unit 1

Grammar builder

Remember ☆☆☆

We add **-ed** to form the past tense of regular verbs.

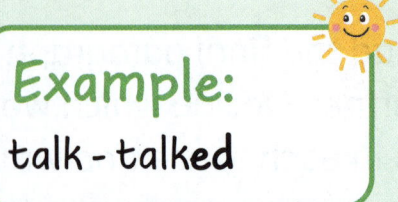

Example:
talk - talk**ed**

1 Change the verbs in the sentences to the past tense.

1 The boy kicks the ball.

   _____

2 Julie boils the water for the tea.

   _____

3 Mom helps me with my reading.

   _____

4 Dad parks the car.

   _____

5 I push the trolley.

   _____

6 They visit Grandma on Sunday.

   _____

Remember

- Use **capital letters** at the beginning of a sentence and for names, places, months and days of the week.
- Use a **full stop** at the end of a sentence.
- Use **commas** to separate things in a sentence.

Example:
My friend Winston went to Kingston market last Saturday. He bought some oranges, apples, bananas and a coconut.

2 Rewrite the sentences with capitals and the correct punctuation.

1. harry lives in negril

   _____

2. there are apples oranges and limes on the table

   _____

3. there is a dance festival on monday in kingston

   _____

4. my birthday is in june

   _____

5. we climbed the sugar loaf mountain yesterday

   _____

6. peter waited at the bus stop

   _____

Term 2 Unit 1

Let's write

1. Work in groups of two or three. Choose a story from one of the pictures below or think of one you know. Make notes about the story. Use the questions to help you.

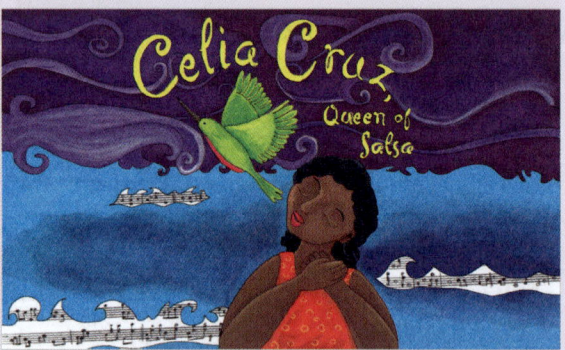
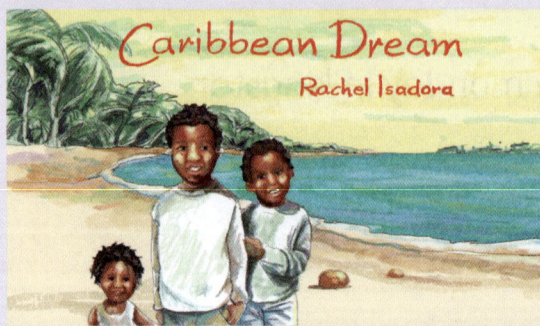
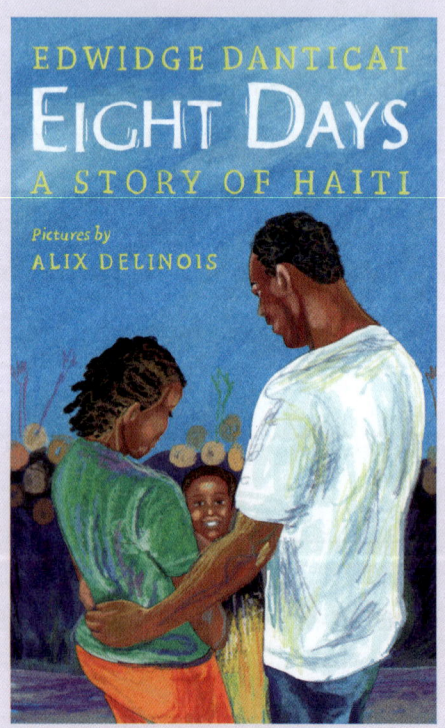

- Who are the main characters? Describe them.
- How does the story begin?
- Where are they?
- What happens?
- How does the story end?

2 Write the story. Use the past tense. When you finish, check your spelling and punctuation.

_____

_____

_____

_____

_____

_____

_____

_____

_____

3 Each person in your group should read a part of the story to the class.

Chapter 15

Speaking and listening

1. Work with your partner. Use the phrases below the pictures to role play the conversations.

Student A: Would you like a sweet?
Student B: Yes, please.

Student A: Would you like some salad?
Student B: I am fine, thank you.

Student A: Let me give you a hand.
Student B: That is very kind of you.

Student A: Would you like some water?
Student B: Yes, please.

2 Walk around the class and ask and answer the questions from the table below with other students.

Offer	Can I help you… ? Let me give you a hand.
Thanks	Thank you. That is very kind of you. Yes, please. No, thank you. I am fine, thank you.

3 Work with a partner. Choose a person in Jamaican culture or history that we should remember and thank for doing something good for Jamaica. Talk about why this person is famous and what this person does or did.

Example:

Harry Belafonte was a Jamaican singer.

He was famous because of his popular songs like *The Banana Boat Song*.

We should remember that he talked about how all people should be equal.

_____ was / is _____.

He / She was famous because _____.

We should thank him / her because _____.

4 Now find another student and tell him or her about the Jamaican person you chose to remember and thank.

Term 2 Unit 1

Word builder

1. Look at the picture and write the word. Circle the sounds *sh*, *ch*, *th*, *ph* in the word.

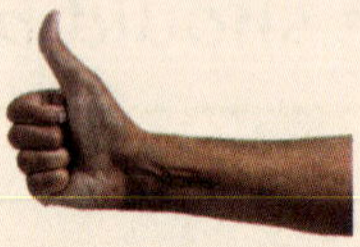

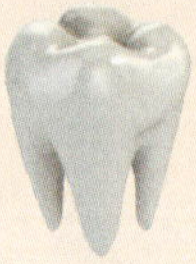

Remember ☆☆☆

Sometimes two consonant letters next to each other make one sound. For example: **sh**ark (at the beginning of the word) or fi**sh** (at the end of the word).

2 Read the poem to yourself. Tell your partner where you think the man is and the reason for your answer.

> I pushed my way through the door
> I am in a rush, but my shoes are new and I cannot run
> Oh, how I wish I got here earlier
> I sit down and the cushion on the chair is plush
> The programme starts and I begin to cough
> The lady next to me tells me to shush
> I look up to the front and even though
> things did not go as planned
> I am still a happy man
> I am still a happy man.

3 With your partner, circle all the *sh* consonant blends. Now read the poem to each other and notice whether the *sh* is at the beginning, the middle or the end of the words when you pronounce the words.

4 Put the words from the poem with *sh* in the correct place in the table.

Beginning	Middle	End	More than one place
	pushed		

145

Let's read

1. Look at the title and the first sentence of the paragraph. What do you think the text will be about?

   ### Swims like a fish

   Winston was only two years old when he could first swim. He is now ten years old and he is Jamaica's youngest swimming champion! Last year he entered the Caribbean national swimming competition and he won first place in the 100 m freestyle.

   Were your predictions right or wrong?

2. Look at the title and the first sentence of the paragraph. What do you think the text will be about?

   ### Student becomes teacher

   Winston is a special swimming teacher. Winston practises swimming every morning and then goes to school. Winston wants other children to learn to swim like he can, so when school finishes, he offers free swimming lessons to his classmates. Winston says he wants to teach children to swim like a fish. He thinks that it is important to share his skill with other children and he enjoys helping others to improve their swimming skill.

   Were your predictions right or wrong?

3 Read the sentences and write true (T) or false (F).

1 Winston was 10 years old when he started to swim. _____

2 Winston was Jamaica's youngest swimmer when he was two years old. _____

3 Winston helps his swimming teacher give swimming lessons to children. _____

4 Winston likes teaching other children to swim well. _____

> **What's your view?**
> Are people good at skills like sport, art or singing because they practise or is this just talent?

4 Use the text to help you answer the questions.

1 Do you think that Winston is a hard worker? Explain your ideas.

_____

2 Is Winston a kind person? Explain how you know.

_____

3 Are you similar to Winston, or different?

_____

Term 2 Unit 1

 Grammar builder

1 Use the table to ask your classmates what they did during the last holiday. Write their name on the line below each activity.

Remember
We add **-ed** to form the past tense of regular verbs.

Example:
You: What did you do during the last holiday?
Alia: I visited my grandparents.
Tom: I spent time with my grandmother.

If your partner says an activity which is not in the table, add it to the table yourself.

Activity	• visited my grandparents _____ _____ _____	• played football _____ _____ _____	• planted a tree _____ _____ _____
Activity	• cleaned my room _____ _____ _____	• went to the beach _____ _____ _____	• cooked a meal _____ _____ _____

Add activity	• _____ _____ _____ _____	• _____ _____ _____ _____	• _____ _____ _____ _____

Look and learn

There are different ways to make negative sentences. To make negative sentences about activities in the past, use **did not**. For example: *Alia **did not** go to the beach. Dean and Lucy **did not** plant a tree.*

2. Work with a partner. Look at the information in your table and write a report on how many students did some of the activities. Report back to the class.

Example:

Alia, Lyon and Anna visited their grandparents. Lyon and Anna went to the beach, but Alia **did not** go to the beach.

Remember ☆☆☆

We use **an** in front of a word starting with a vowel (a, e, i, o, u) and **a** in front of a word starting with a consonant (b, c, d, f, g…).

3 Work with a partner. Fill in *a* or *an* in the sentences and tell your partner why you chose *a* or *an*. For example: "I chose *a* because the word *cat* begins with a consonant".

1. This is ____ cat.

2. Here is ____ egg.

3. This is ____ arm and ____ leg.

4. There is ____ ball in the road.

5. Here is ____ picture.

6. Mom has ____ orange.

7. Dad wants ____ banana.

8. We went on ____ aeroplane.

Chapter 15

Let's write

1. Work in groups of two or three. Choose a story from Jamaican history. It could be about:
   - a famous person, such as Bob Marley
   - an important time in Jamaican history, for example when Usain Bolt broke three world records in the 2008 Olympics for Jamaica
   - a story that your grandparents or parents have told you.

2. Plan the story. Use the questions to help you. Write notes on the organiser below.
   - Who are the characters in the story?
   - How does the story begin?
   - What happens next?
   - How does the story end?

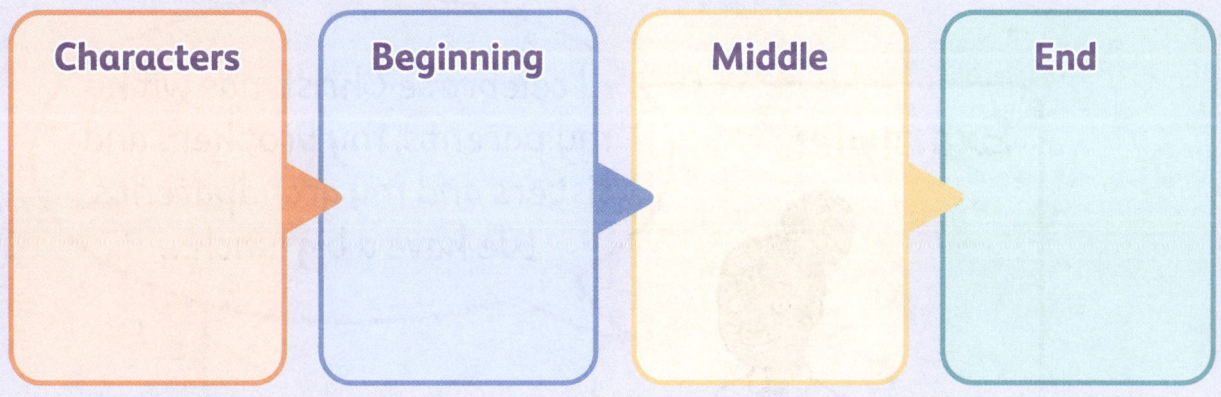

3. Write the story. Use the past tense.

4. When you finish, as a group, check your spelling and punctuation. Revise any sentences you are not happy about and, as a group, write out your draft in your best handwriting.

Chapter 16

Speaking and listening

1. Work with your partner. Look at the pictures about celebrations. Ask and answer the questions for each picture.
   - Who do you celebrate with?
   - How do you celebrate?
   - Do you like this celebration? Why? Why not?

We celebrate Christmas.

We celebrate our birthday.

We celebrate sports.

Example:

I celebrate Christmas with my parents, my brothers and sisters and my grandparents. We have a big lunch...

2. What other events do you celebrate with your family and friends?

3. Work with your partner. Talk about all the people you should thank for making the celebration a success. For example: *I think I should thank my mom for Christmas because she cooks our Christmas dinner.*

Chapter 16

Word builder

> **Look and learn**
> Some words sound the same, but are spelled differently and have different meanings. For example: *there / their*. These words are called **homophones**.

1 Draw a line to match the words that sound the same. Then colour them with the same colour.

- there — their
- hear
- for
- eight
- here
- two
- four
- one
- meat
- ate
- board
- bored
- won
- too
- meet

Term 2 Unit 1

2 Listen to your teacher read the sentences. Then complete the sentences with the correct word from Activity 1.

1 We usually eat _____ at Christmas.

2 I like to play _____ games on Christmas day with my family.

3 Henry got a gold medal because he _____ the race.

4 _____ are five people in my family.

5 Can you _____ the birds singing in the trees?

6 I _____ lots of cake at my birthday party.

Chapter 16

Let's read

1 Read the text and complete the sentences.

Clive is ten years old and he is already an athletics champion! Clive was in a national competition last month and he won first place in the 200 m and 400 m races. He also came first in the hurdles. Clive celebrated with his family. He always celebrates happy times with them. They all went out for dinner at Clive's favourite restaurant. His parents gave him some money as a present.

Clive started running in races when he was just four. He wanted to be like his older brother Isaac. Isaac was the best in his school at running. He competed in many national competitions and he won lots of prizes, but his dream was not to be an athlete – he wanted to be a doctor. Isaac's dream came true when he got a place at a university.

When Isaac left for university, Clive was sad. He missed his brother and he did not have anyone to train with. Isaac wrote to his little brother often and he told him to keep training and become a great athlete, so Clive kept working hard. During his last competition a famous coach saw Clive run. This coach wants to train with him and make him a champion. Clive is very happy about this and so is Isaac. Soon Clive will become the next Usain Bolt!

1 How old is Clive? He _____.

2 What did Clive win last month. He _____.

3 How did Clive and his family celebrate? They went _____.

4 Who did Clive want to be like? He _____.

5 What was Isaac's dream? He wanted _____.

2 Circle the correct answer.
   1 What do you think Clive's personality is like?
      a hardworking   b lazy
   2 Who does Clive celebrate important events with?
      a Usain Bolt   b Isaac   c his family
   3 How did Clive feel when Isaac left?
      a happy   b sad   c tired
   4 Who did Clive see at his last competition?
      a his parents   b a famous coach c Isaac

156

Grammar builder

L👀k and learn

A sentence should have **a subject**. For example:

a person	place	a thing
the boy / he	Kingston / it	my books / they

A sentence should have a verb, which describes the subject or what the subject does. For example:

describes the subject	describes what the subject does
The boy is a footballer.	The boy kicks the ball.

1 Read the sentences and circle the subject.
1. He won first place in the race.
2. They went to a restaurant to celebrate.
3. Kingston is a town in Jamaica.
4. The coach wants to train with him.
5. We played cricket last week.
6. The child watched TV.

L👀k and learn

A sentence must have **a subject** and a verb to be complete. For example:
The dog chased the cat.

2 Decide if the phrase is a complete (C) or incomplete (I) sentence. Write "C" or "I".

1 Played football. _____

2 She listened to music. _____

3 We arrived late at school. _____

4 I jumped over the wall. _____

5 Carried the baby. _____

6 An interesting story. _____

3 Write three sentences of your own about a family tradition. For example: *At Christmas we go to carol services. Last year, we sang in church.*

Word box

family   meal   party   celebrate

Use the words in the word box to help you.

_____

_____

_____

_____

_____

_____

Chapter 16

Let's write

1. Choose an event from the list below to write about. Compare your ideas and ask your partner what event they chose and why.

   birthday   Christmas   Easter   graduation

   winning a competition   a wedding

2. Draw a picture of what you did at the event or make a picture from using images from magazines.

3 Answer the questions about the event. Write complete sentences.

1 What was the event? _____

2 When was it? _____

3 Where did it happen? _____

4 Who were you with? _____

5 How did you celebrate it? _____

6 What clothes did you wear? _____

7 What food did you eat? _____

8 What did you do? _____

9 How did you feel? _____

10 What was your favourite thing about the event?

_____

4 Now write about the event.

5 When you finish, compare your writing with your partner and check each other's work for neat handwriting and correct punctuation.

Chapter 17

Speaking and listening

1. Work with your partner. Take turns to read the poem.

Clap your hands
Clap your hands
It is your birthday
It is your special day
All your friends are here
They want to hear you laughing
Because it is your birthday
Let us cut your cake
Let us dance and shake
Everyone sing "happy birthday to you".

Clap your hands
Clap your hands
It is your birthday
It is your special day
Let us go outside and play
All your friends are there with their party clothes
Look! There are some gifts on a chair
You have two cars
And a book too
Everyone sing "happy birthday to you".

2   Now take turns to role play the actions in the poem as you read it.

3   Work with your partner. Ask and answer questions about your birthday.

Student A: How old are you?

Student B: I am _____ years old.

Student A: When were you born?

Student B: I was born _____.

> **Example:**
> I was born on the 4th of October, 2013.

> **What's your view?**
> Is it rude to ask an older person their age? Why? Why not?

Chapter 17

Word builder

> **Remember** ☆☆☆
>
> **Homophones** are words that sound the same, but have a different meaning and spelling. For example: *buy / bye*.

1 Can you find any homophones in the poem in the "Speaking and listening" lesson? Write them below and say the words to your partner. Then match the words that sound the same. For example: *one / won*.

_____

2 Say the words. Then draw a line to match them to the pictures.

1 one

2 hare

3 won

4 hair

5 blue

6 blew

163

3 Complete the sentences with the words in the word box.

Word box

| be | flower | him | night |
| bee | flour | hymn | knight |

1 The _____ is flying around my head!

2 Last night when we were at church we sang my favourite _____.

3 The forest is scary at _____ because it is very dark.

4 The _____ put his sword on the table.

5 Errol wants to _____ a footballer when he grows up.

6 Jason wants a laptop for his birthday so I got one for _____.

7 We used _____ to make the cake.

8 My mom cut a _____ from the garden and put it in a vase.

Chapter 17

Let's read

L👀k and learn

We send **invitations** for special events like birthday parties.

It is a **birthday party!**

You are invited to my party on Saturday 14th May at 1 p.m.

It is a fancy-dress party, the theme is superheroes, so please wear a costume.

There will be a competition for the best costume. The winner gets a fantastic gift!

After the fancy dress competition, there will be a big lunch!

We also have a band and a DJ, so do not forget to bring your dancing shoes.

There will also be lots of fun games to play.

I hope you can come to my party. Can you please complete the RSVP slip below and send it back to me, so I know how many people are coming? The party is at my house. My address is 42 Seymour Road.

Thank you!

Donovan

✂ -

RSVP   Donovan's party
I am coming. ☐   I cannot come. ☐

Term 2 Unit 1

1   Read the invitation and answer the questions.

   1   What is Donovan celebrating?
       _____

   2   What date is the party on?
       _____

   3   What time is the party?
       _____

   4   Where is the party?
       _____

   5   What kind of costumes will people wear to the party?
       _____

   6   What other activities will there be at the party?
       _____

   7   What do you think an RSVP is?
       _____

Grammar builder

L👀k and learn

A **subject** can be just one word such as *David* or a pronoun such as *he*.

A **subject** can be two (or more) words such as *Lynda and Jane*, or a noun phrase such as *the winner of the competition*.

Subject	Verb	Object / Complement
The winner	gets	a fantastic gift.

1 Circle the subject in the sentences.
1. David was tired after the football match.
2. They went to the party on Saturday.
3. The boys played computer games.
4. Alison and Jenny decided to go to the beach.
5. The dog chased the cat.
6. We skated in the park.

L👀k and learn

We use **pronouns** to avoid repeating the same nouns in a sentence or paragraph. For example: *Jack plays tennis with his friends.* **He (Jack)** *likes playing tennis.*

2 Read the paragraphs below. Use pronouns to avoid repeating the underlined subjects too often in the paragraphs.

1 The children and Lukas went to a party on Saturday. <u>The children</u> played games at the party and <u>the children</u> also watched a movie called Finding Dory; <u>the movie</u> was very funny.

_____

_____

_____

_____

2 <u>Lucas</u> won a prize at school for being the best student and <u>Lucas</u> was very happy. <u>Lucas</u> got a medal and a new book. After <u>Lucas</u> got the prize <u>Lucas</u> went out for dinner with <u>Lucas's</u> family. <u>The family</u> went to a nice restaurant to celebrate.

_____

_____

_____

_____

Chapter 17

Let's write

1. Write an invitation to a birthday party. Use the words in the word box to help you. Decorate your card.

Word box

| invited | food | dance | send |
| games | music | party | RSVP |

Remember ☆☆☆

- Include the date, time and place of the party.
- Write about any fun activities at the party and what else there will be at the party.
- Ask your guest to RSVP, so you know if they are coming.

Dear _____,

You are _____

Time: _____

Place: _____

There will be …

_____

2. When you finish, compare your invitation with your partner's and check each other's work for neat handwriting and correct punctuation.

169

Chapter 18

Speaking and listening

1. In pairs, take turns to read aloud the example text about relaxing. Draw a picture of your favourite way to relax.

Example:

> I relax by putting my headphones on and listening to music on my phone. I sit in a nice big chair in my bedroom and all I can hear is the beat of the music. I do this alone, but sometimes my little sister wants to play with me, so I remove my headphones and let her listen to the music with me.

2. Work with your partner. Ask and answer the questions below.
    1. What do you do to relax?
    2. Where do you relax?
    3. Who do you relax with?

3. In groups of four, look at the example in Activity 1 to guide you and tell your group what you do to relax.

Chapter 18

Word builder

Look and learn

Homographs are words that have the same spelling, but have different meanings.

Example:

We turn on the **light** at night.
A feather is very **light**.

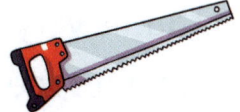

He used a **saw** to cut the board.
I **saw** my friend after school.

The sun began to **sink** in the west.
I washed my hands in the **sink**.
We went to the **park**.
My mom has to **park** the car.

1 Choose the correct meaning from the next page for each underlined word. Write the correct letters (a to h) next to the sentences 1 to 8.
   1 I like to <u>watch</u> TV in the evenings. ____
   2 My hair is not thick, it is very <u>fine</u>. ____
   3 There is a <u>tear</u> in my trousers. ____
   4 Henry is playing with the <u>bat</u> and ball. ____
   5 Deborah got a new <u>watch</u> for her birthday. ____
   6 My dad paid a <u>fine</u> because he parked his car in the wrong place. ____
   7 There were <u>tears</u> in the old woman's eyes when she saw her grandchildren. ____
   8 It was Mike's turn to <u>bat</u>. ____

171

a   something you use to tell the time
b   a rip in a material like clothes
c   water that comes from the eyes when a person is sad
d   something you use to hit a ball
e   money a person has to pay when they do something against the law
f   to look at a show, a movie, or drama
g   something that is very thin
h   when a person hits the ball in a cricket or baseball game

2   Complete the story with the homographs from the word box. The words will be used more than once.

Word box

watch   match   sign

In his free time Jason likes to ¹_____ cricket. Last week Jason and his friends went to a cricket ²_____. After the game Jason went to meet some of the players. One of the players decided to ³_____ the ball with his name and gave it to Jason. Jason was very happy.

Later Jason and his friends went to the park. They had some food and wanted to eat. They saw a ⁴_____ for the picnic area and went to sit there. After a while Jason looked at his ⁵_____ and could see it was late. The boys decided it was time to go home. But now it was quite dark and there were no lights. Jason had some candles in his bag so they lit a ⁶_____ and used it to light some candles. Finally, the boys found their way out of the park.

Let's read

Remember ☆☆☆

We use **similes** in poems to compare two things in an interesting way. **Similes** use the words *like* or *as... as*. For example: *He swims **like** a fish. She is **as** light **as** a feather.*

1   1   Read the poem. How many times does the writer use similes?

_____

Relaxing feels…
like the warm sun on my skin
like the birds singing
like my mother's cooking
like the salt of the sea on my lips
like my grandmother's smile.

Relaxing is…
as nice as walking on sand
as funny as my friend telling a joke
as fresh as baked bread in the air
as sweet as honey
as beautiful as rows of sunflowers waving in the breeze.

2   Underline all of the similes in the poem.
3   Which simile do you like best? Discuss it with your partner.

2 Which words or phrases from the poem do you think describe the following senses? Write them below. The first one is done for you.

  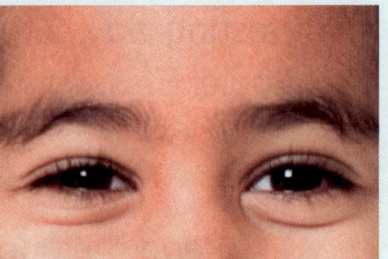

touch   hearing   sight

<u>like the warm</u>   _____   _____

<u>sun on my skin</u>   _____   _____

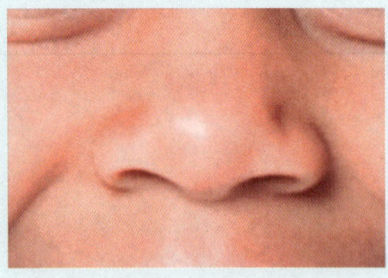 

smell   taste

_____   _____

_____   _____

3 Think of examples of your own experience of the senses in Activity 2. You could think about a place that you have visited, or a special day that you remember. Use similes to tell your partner about these experiences.

Grammar builder

Remember ☆☆☆

Pronouns can be used to replace nouns in sentences.

1 Replace the underlined word or words with pronouns from the word box.

Word box

She   She   Her   her   they   they

Sarah likes to read books in her leisure time. ¹Sarah's _____ favourite books are the Harry Potter series. ²Sarah _____ loves Harry Potter! Last year when Sarah's family went to Florida, ³Sarah's _____ family visited the Harry Potter theme park. Sarah really enjoyed the trip.

Sarah also likes to draw. Drawing makes ⁴Sarah _____ feel relaxed. ⁵Sarah _____ likes to meet her friends in her free time. Sometimes ⁶Sarah and her friends _____ go to the cinema.

Remember

- Use a **capital letter** at the beginning of a sentence and for names, places and the pronoun "I".
- Use **full stops** at the end of sentences.
- Use **commas** for lists.

2 Rewrite the paragraph below with the correct punctuation.

my name is jack and i am seven years old in my free time i like to play sports i play football cricket and basketball i am good at football i also like to play computer games they are fun sometimes i play with my friends frank sally and adam

_____

_____

_____

_____

_____

_____

Chapter 18

Let's write

1. Work in groups of three or four.
   - What is the person called who writes a poem?
   - Read the information on what makes a good poem. In your group think of examples for each point.

   A poem:
   - uses imaginative words
   - shares ideas and emotions
   - has words or phrases that sound good together
   - can rhyme
   - does not have to rhyme!

2. Think about your senses: hearing, taste, sight, touch and smell. Write a sentence about how you use your senses.

Example:
Hearing – When I listen to music it is like I am having a party.

Taste – _____

Sight – _____

Touch – _____

Smell – _____

Check your spelling and punctuation. Have you started your sentences with a capital letter? Have you used commas? Have you used full stops?

Compare your sentences with your partner.

Remember ☆☆☆

We use **as ... as** and **like** in similes to compare things. For example:

*Reggae music is **as** happy **as** the sun.*
*Reggae sounds **like** the weekend.*

3 Write a short poem using similes *as ... as* and *like* about how you relax. Look at the poem *Relaxing feels…* in the "Let's read" lesson to guide you. Look at your sentences in Activity 2 for ideas.

_____

_____

_____

_____

4 When you finish, read your poem aloud to hear how it sounds.

Term 2 Unit 1 Review and assessment

Speaking and listening

1   Think of a time you went to a special place. Tell your partner.

- Who was there?

  <u>I went to the beach with my family.</u>

- What happened?

  _____

- When did it happen?

  _____

- Where did it happen?

  _____

- Why did it happen?

  _____

Word builder

> **Remember** ☆☆☆
>
> A **consonant blend** is usually two consonants that blend together, but <u>each sound can still be heard</u>. For example: *cl*oud, *bl*ack.
>
> A **consonant digraph** is two letters next to each other that makes <u>one sound</u>. For example: *sh*ark, fi*sh*.

179

Term 2 Unit 1

1 Place the words in the word box under consonant blend or consonant digraph.

Word box

~~chair~~	shoe	whale	sleep
~~clock~~	fish	blue	glove
photograph	thumb	skirt	black

Consonant blend	Consonant digraph
clock	chair

 Let's read

A school trip to Dolphin Cove!

Come on the school trip on Friday 5th June from 9 a.m. to 4 p.m.

Go swimming with the dolphins. Get close to three dolphins and feed them. Children from Grade 2 and Grade 3 can go on the trip alone, but children from Grade 1 can only go with a parent.

We will visit Ocho Rios where you can do many activities from playing with the dolphins to learning about their life. This is one place you will definitely have fun while you learn.

Review and assessment

> Get all the answers correct on a quiz and you can enter the competition to win a prize! After the competition there are fun games to play. Finally, there is a big lunch!
>
> If you want to go please complete the form with your parents' signature and give it to your teacher.

1 Read the information on the school trip and answer the questions.
   1. Where is the school trip?
   2. What time will you leave for the school trip?
   3. How many dolphins can you feed?
   4. How can Grade 1 students go on the trip?
   5. How do you enter the competition?

Grammar builder

Make questions using the verbs *to do*, *to have* and *to be*. For example: *Do you like bananas? Do you have a dog? Is this your book?*

1 Reorder the words to make questions. Remember to start your questions with a capital letter.

   1. this / your / book / is?

   _____

   2. you / eat / meat / do?

   _____

   3. is / that / coat / your?

   _____

4 Lloyd does / in / Kingston / live?

_____

5 he / does / have / dog / a?

_____

Let's write

1 Write about what you did for your last birthday. Answer the questions and write complete sentences.

1 When was it? _____

2 Where did it happen? _____

3 Who were you with? _____

4 How did you celebrate it? _____

5 What clothes did you wear? _____

6 What food did you eat? _____

7 What did you do? _____

8 How did you feel? _____

9 What was your favourite thing about the day?

_____

Unit 2

Chapter 19

Speaking and listening

litter on
a beach

pollution
in a river

recycling
plastic bottles

cutting
down trees

switching off
the lights

leaving the
water tap on

cleaning up
the park

planting trees
and flowers

Remember ☆☆☆

- When it is your turn give your opinion.
- Speak clearly.
- Listen carefully.

183

1   Work with your partner and ask and answer the questions below.
    1   What can you see in the pictures?
    2   What is happening in these places?
    3   Is it good or bad for the environment? Why?
    4   Do you do any of the activities in the pictures?

> **What's your view?**
> If we drop sweet papers on the floor, does this really affect the environment?

2   Can you think of other ways to help the environment?

Chapter 19

Word builder

Look and learn
Words are broken down to parts that each contains one vowel. These parts are called **syllables**. A syllable can be a sound or a beat. Short words may have just one or two syllables, but longer words can have more. The best way to recognise syllables is to say a word out loud, slowly. For example, when we say *pollution*, we can break it down into these syllables: po*llu*tion. How many syllables are there in this word?

1 Say the words and write the number of syllables. If you are not sure, use a dictionary or online tool to check the number of syllables in the words.

1 recycle _____   2 protect _____

3 environment _____   4 conservation _____

5 plastic _____   6 cardboard _____

7 paper _____   8 reuse _____

2 Match the pictures to the words.

1 environment   2 climate change   3 pollution
4 waste   5 recycle   6 protect

185

Let's read

1 Read Shirley's blog and answer the questions.

Shirley's Blog

11 May 2021

Blue Mountains Park Adventure

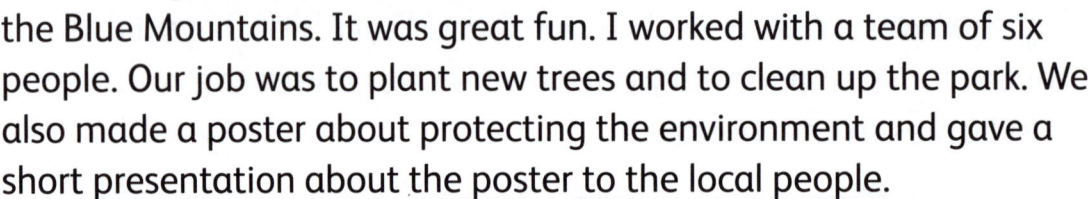

Hello! It is Shirley again back with my blog. Sorry I did not write anything for two weeks, I was doing some conservation work in the Blue Mountains. It was great fun. I worked with a team of six people. Our job was to plant new trees and to clean up the park. We also made a poster about protecting the environment and gave a short presentation about the poster to the local people.

We planted coffee trees in the park. This was fun. I really enjoyed planting trees. We also removed harmful plants from the park. These plants are called invasive plants.

It was a great experience. I enjoyed the work and I made some great friends. Anyone who wants to help with the conservation work can call John on 01822 35684.

1 Why did Shirley not post for two weeks? She was doing _____.

2 How did Shirley feel about the work she did? She thought it was _____.

3 What was the poster about? The poster was about _____.

4 What are invasive plants? Invasive plants are _____.

5 If you want to do conservation work at the park who can you contact? _____.

Grammar builder

> **Look and learn**
> A **proper noun**, like a person's name, or the name of a town or a place, begins with a capital letter.

1 Look at Shirley's blog in the "Let's read" lesson. All her sentences start with capital letters, but there are other words and phrases in the blog that also start with capital letters. What are they? Write them below.

_____ _____ _____

What do we call these words and phrases? Check the "Look and learn" box for the answer.

2 Read the sentences and rewrite them with the correct punctuation.

1. it is important to recycle plastic bottles

   _____

2. you can reuse things to make art

   _____

3. james picks up litter at negril beach montego bay and sandy bay

   _____

4 sally always switches off the lights when she goes to bed

_____

5 we do conservation projects in jamaica

_____

Spelling

3 Unscramble and write the words from the word box.

Word box		
environment	pollution	recycle
litter	conservation	plastic
forest	waste	

1 tnlioulpo   _____

2 mnnnvieoter   _____

3 stnnoecoivar   _____

4 osfrte   _____

5 rycclee   _____

6 iatpslc   _____

7 eilttr   _____

8 taswe   _____

Chapter 19

Let's write

1. Look at the picture.
   - What can you see?
   - What is happening?

2. Use the picture, the underlined headings and the sentences to make up a story in the past. Think about:

   The characters: There were two boys called James and Bob. They were both 8 years old.

   _____

   The place: They were at the beach. It was a lovely day.

   _____

   _____

   What is the story about? James and Bob wanted to help keep Jamaica clean. So, they went to the beach. When they got to the beach, they were surprised because…

   _____

   _____

   _____

   What does it look like? _____

   What does it smell like? _____

3. Now ask your partner about their story.

189

Ask the following questions:
- Who are the characters?
- What do they look like?
- How old are they?
- Where are they?
- What are they doing?
- What problem do they have?
- How do they solve it?
- What happens in the end?

Remember ☆☆☆
Check your spelling, grammar and punctuation.

4 Now write your story below.

_____
_____
_____
_____
_____
_____
_____
_____

5 When you finish, check your spelling and punctuation. Have you started your sentences with a capital letter? Have you used commas and full stops? Compare your sentences with your partner.

Chapter 20

Speaking and listening

1. Work with your partner. Look at the pictures of the life cycle of a plant. Put the pictures in order and write the correct number in the box. Check the order with your teacher.

2. Take turns with your partner to describe the life cycle of a plant. Use the sequence words in the word box to help you.

Word box

First   then   next   after that   finally

3 Work with a partner. Choose a plant to describe to the class. It can be a flower or a vegetable. Go online or to the library to find out information. Think about its colour, size and how it grows.

When I speak...

- ☐ I speak clearly.
- ☐ I look at my audience.
- ☐ I speak so I can be heard.
- ☐ I speak slowly.
- ☐ I answer questions that are asked.
- ☐ I stand / sit still.

Word builder

1 Help the frog get across the pond. Say the words. Then colour in the words that use the same letters to make a sound with the same colour. There are four different sets of letters that make sounds so use four different colours.

Remember ☆☆☆

Say the sounds out loud. What sounds do you hear?
ow as in *blow, crow, window*
ou as in *count, cloud, loud*
oi as in *soil, point, noise*
oy as in *boy, toy, joy*

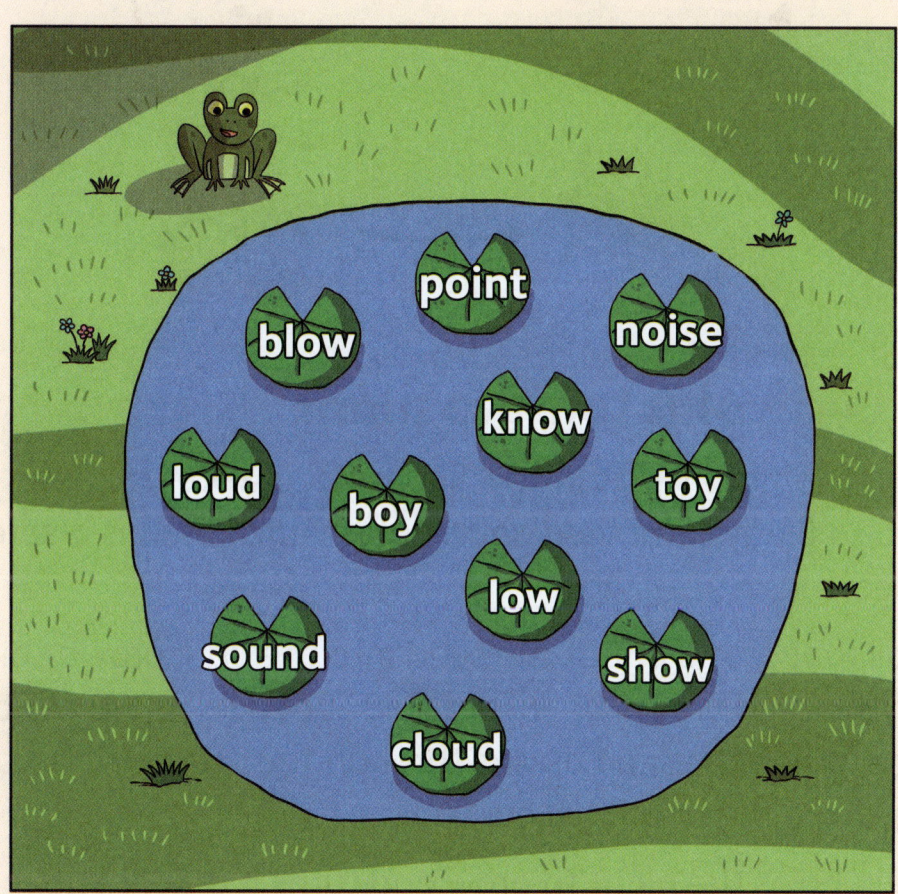

2 Work with a partner. Take turns to say and spell the words in the pond.

3 You and your partner take turns to pick a word from the "Look and learn" box or from the pond, but do not tell your partner which word. Spell the word out loud. Your partner should say the word.

Let's read

Read the text and answer the questions.

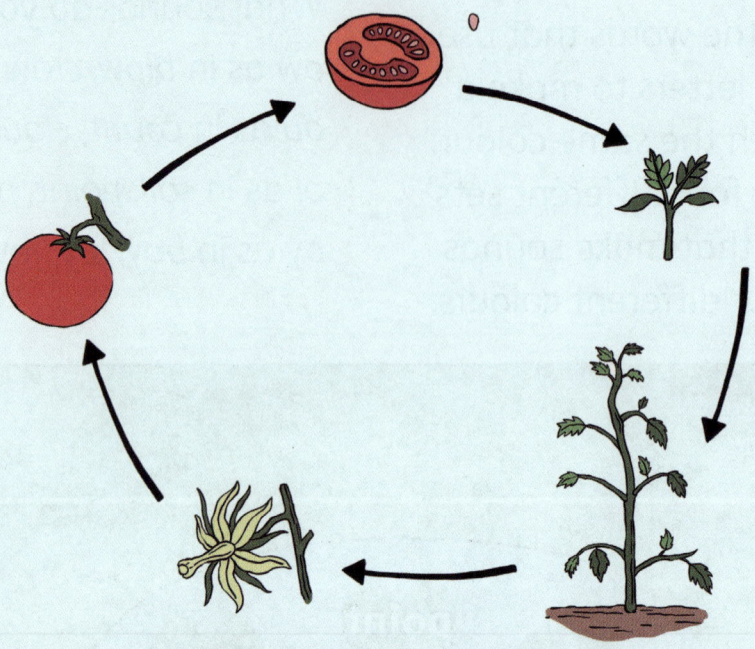

Life cycle of a tomato plant

We plant tomato seeds in soil. Seeds need water to grow. After 5 to 6 days, the seed germinates which means it sprouts and becomes a seedling.

A small root grows out of the seed into the dark brown soil. When the seed breaks open, the sprout begins its way to the surface. When the seed breaks through the ground, it gets energy from the bright yellow Sun.

The Sun helps the plant to grow and turns it green. The root of the plant helps bring food from the soil and the stem takes it to all parts of the plant. The plant then makes its own food in the leaves to help the plant to grow.

Plants make oxygen which is the same as air. People breathe oxygen and need it to live. Plants are also used by people for food, so plants are very important for people.

1   Circle the correct answer for each question.

   1   What do plants grow from?

      a   the sun   b   the air   c   seeds

   2   How long does it take the seed to become a seedling?

      a   5 days   b   5 to 6 days   c   6 days

   3   Where do plants get energy from?

      a   water   b   the Sun   c   seeds

   4   What colour does the Sun make the plant?

      a   green   b   yellow   c   brown

   5   What does the root of the plant do?

      a   helps bring food from the soil

      b   helps bring food from the Sun

      c   helps bring food from the seed

2   Is this a fiction text (like a story), or a non-fiction text (a text with facts)? Explain how you know.

   _____

   _____

Grammar builder

L👀k and learn
How do we form the plural of regular nouns?

root**s**   tree**s**   bucket**s**

Some nouns are **irregular** and have a different spelling for plurals. For example:

leaf – leaves

branch – branches

box – boxes

butterfly – butterflies

1 Write the plural form of the nouns. Some are irregular.

1   tomato   _____

2   seed   _____

3   plant   _____

4   leaf   _____

5   knife   _____

6   plant   _____

7   shelf   _____

8   berry   _____

9   fruit   _____

10 flower   _____

> **Remember** ☆☆☆
> - We use a **comma** in a sentence when we have a list of more than three things.
> - We use a **full stop** at the end of a sentence.

2. Add commas and full stops to the sentences.
   1. I need soil water seeds and a spade to grow plants
   2. Jake grows tomatoes cucumbers onions and potatoes in his vegetable garden
   3. Plants need light water and soil to grow
   4. In our school we grow mangoes oranges apples and grapefruits
   5. Helen has a beautiful garden with lots of flowers trees and plants
   6. There are apples pears and cherry trees in the farm.

Let's write

1. Look at the text in the "Let's read" lesson. What verb tense does the writer use?

2. Choose one of the plants below. Draw and write a life cycle for it. Use the internet to find out information about the plant and the sentences below to help you.

sunflower   apple tree   sugar cane   bean

Life cycle of a _____

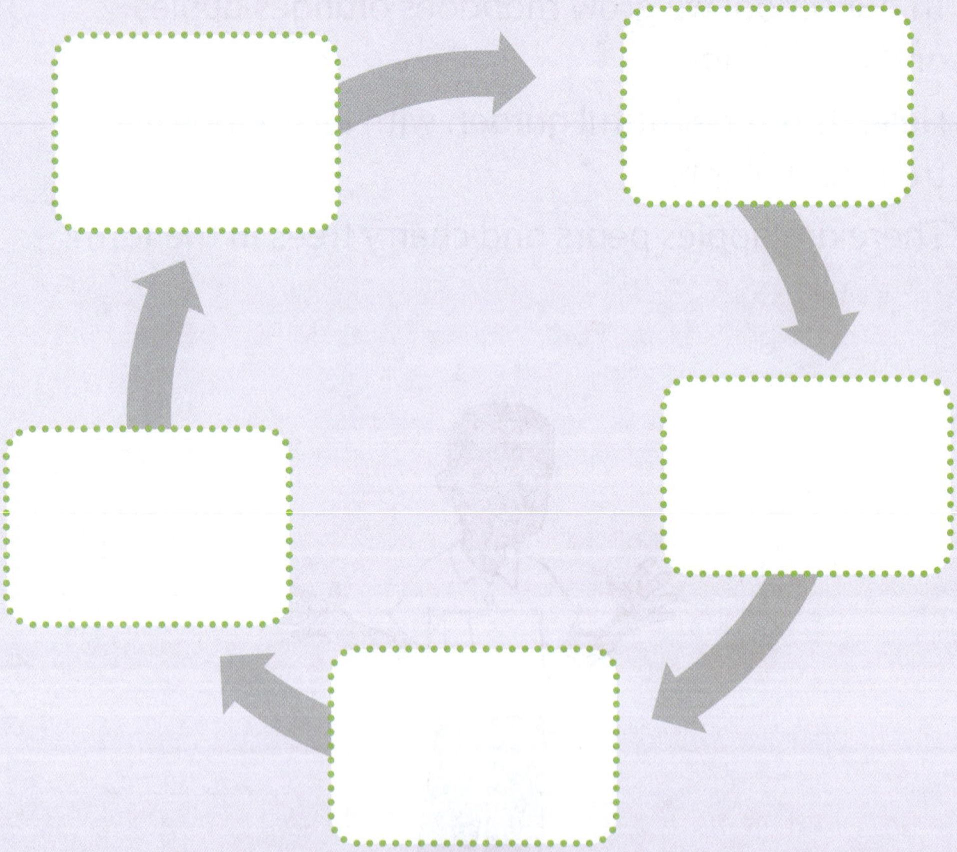

We plant ¹_____ seeds in soil.

²_____ need water to grow.

After ³_____ days, the ⁴_____ begins to grow. Small roots grow into soil.

The plant gets energy from ⁵_____.

The sun helps the plant to grow and turns it green.

Chapter 21

Speaking and listening

1. Look at the pictures. Then listen to your teacher tell the story. How did the donkey help the farmer and his son?

2 In groups of three, role play one of the pictures for your group to guess. Mime the nouns in the pictures. Use the nouns and phrases in the word box to help you.

> **Word box**
>
> | | | |
> |---|---|---|
> | a man | a wheelbarrow | a red hat |
> | a little boy | a donkey | a blue hat |
> | sugar cane | a cart | |

Term 2 Unit 2

Word builder

1 Look at the pictures. Say the word then complete the crossword.

Look and learn

Some words have **silent letters**. For example, what is the silent letter in the word *knife*?

Down

Across

1 3  6

2  4  7

6  5

					¹t		
	²w		³w		a	t	
⁴	n	i	g		t		u
			a				m
			⁵l	a			
⁶	n	i	f				
n							
⁷c	o	m					
c							
k							

202

Chapter 21

Let's read

1 Read the text. Match the headings in the word box to the gaps 1-6.

Word box

Work   Food (x2)   Pets   Clothes   Transport

1 _____

Cows, sheep and goats give us milk and cheese. Farmers get milk from these animals. We drink milk and use it in our food. Farmers can also make cheese from the milk.

2 _____

Cows, sheep and goats give us leather. Sheep also give us wool. We use wool to make warm clothes.

3 _____

Chickens and ducks give us eggs. We cook with eggs.

4 _____

Animals like donkeys, horses and camels help us move things from one place to a another. Camels live in the desert; they can walk 100 miles in a day while carrying heavy loads. Horses can carry people from one place to another.

203

5 _____

Animals like the buffalo and ox help us with our work on the farm. They help the farmers to plough the fields so the crops can grow.

6 _____

Animals are also our friends. We look after them and they give us their love. Dogs can also protect our homes from burglars.

2 Read the text. Answer the questions.
1 Which animals give us something we can drink?
2 Which animals produce wool?
3 Where do camels live?
4 How do the buffalo and ox help people?

3 What would be a good title for this text? Share your ideas with a partner.

Grammar builder

Remember ☆☆☆

- We make a regular noun plural by adding **-s**. What is the plural form of *chicken*?
- **Irregular plural nouns** have different rules which is good to learn and remember. What is the plural form of *knife*?

1 Look at the plural nouns. Find and correct spelling mistakes. If the spelling is correct, write "C".

1 boxs _____

2 duckes _____

3 cows _____

4 pigs _____

5 tomatos _____

6 foxes _____

7 potatos _____

8 horses _____

9 dogs _____

10 sandwichs _____

2 Add punctuation (capital letters, commas and full stops) to the sentences.

> **Remember** ☆ ☆ ☆
> - Use a **capital letter** at the beginning of a sentence and for names, places and the pronoun "I".
> - Use **commas** for lists.
> - Use **full stops** at the end of sentences.

1 there are pigs sheep cow horses and chickens on the farm
2 we make cheese from goat's milk
3 i have a dog a cat and a rabbit
4 harry works on a farm in the summer months
5 my dad grows sugar cane corn and sunflowers
6 my grandparents have a farm in manchester parish

Let's write

1. Think of ways animals help humans. Use the ideas below to help you write a few notes.
   - to do work on farms
   - to give us food
   - to give us clothes
   - to transport things
   - to help a blind person to move around
   - to be our friends

2. Draw a picture of an animal helping a person to do something.

3 Write a paragraph about the animal you drew in Activity 2 and how it helps the person.

> **Example:**
> The cow lives on a farm. It eats grass and gives us milk. We also get meat from cows.

_____

_____

_____

_____

_____

_____

_____

Chapter 22

Speaking and listening

1. Look at the pictures. Then listen to your teacher tell the story. How did the mouse help the lion?

The Lion and the Mouse

2. In pairs, take turns to ask and answer questions about the story. Think about the question words – *Where*, *What*, *When*, *Why* and *How* – and use the words and phrases in the word box to help you.

Example: Where was the lion sleeping?

He was sleeping under the tree.

Word box

- was sleeping
- was scared
- was growling
- was caught in a net
- was biting and chewing on the net
- was kissing and saying thank you to the mouse

3. With your partner, discuss the following question: What lesson do you think the lion learned at the end of the story?

What's your view?
What is more important, helping other students or getting your work finished first?

Word builder

1 Say the words then write it under the correct sound *ou* or *ow*. The first one in each sound is done for you.

ou words

1 <u>count</u>
2 _____
3 _____
4 _____
5 _____
6 _____
7 _____
8 _____

ow words

1 <u>how</u>
2 _____
3 _____
4 _____
5 _____
6 _____
7 _____
8 _____

2 Choose a word from the *ou* and the *ow* groups and write a sentence for each word. Read the sentence to your partner and ask your partner to identify if the word is an *ou* or *ow* word.

Example:

210

Let's read

1 Read the story. Match the words from the story to their meanings.

1 boast
2 tease
3 stubby
4 nap
5 tiptoe
6 worried

a to walk slowly and quietly
b to go to sleep
c to say you are great at doing something
d nervous
e to make fun of someone
f fat

The Hare and the Tortoise

There once was a hare who would boast about how he was the best at running. He talked about how fast he could run. He did this all day long to his friend, tortoise. The hare had slim legs and could run fast. Tortoise had short legs and could not run, but only walk slowly. It took tortoise a long time to get anywhere. Hare always teased and laughed at tortoise about how slowly he walked. One day, the tortoise was tired of being teased and hearing about how fast the hare could run, so he challenged hare to a race.

All the animals in the land came to watch the race. Most people believed that hare would win the race because he was always telling everyone how fast he could run.

"Tortoise, you need to run faster to win the race! You are going too slowly!"

The hare decided to go for a nap. He believed the tortoise would take a very long time to finish the race. The hare went for a long sleep.

The tortoise saw that hare was sleeping and he tiptoed past hare. The tortoise smiled because he knew he was going to win the race.

The hare woke up with all the noise from the animals who cheered for the tortoise as he passed the finish line. He looked around, but he could not see the tortoise. He felt worried, he did not know how much time had passed since he saw the tortoise. So he got up and started running.

When the hare arrived at the finish line, he saw that the tortoise had won the race. He looked at tortoise angrily. The animals clapped and cheered for the tortoise.

2   Answer the questions.
    1   Who are the characters in the story?
    2   What did the hare always tease the tortoise about?
    3   How did it make the tortoise feel when the hare teased him?
    4   Why did the hare go for a sleep?
    5   How did the tortoise avoid waking up the hare?
    6   Who won the race?

3   What do you think?
    1   Can a tortoise and a hare race in real life?
    2   What do you think is the message of the story?
    3   How would you feel if someone teased you like the hare teased the tortoise?

4   Work with your partner. Imagine one of you is the tortoise and one of you is the hare. Talk about how you felt from the beginning to the end of the race.

Term 2 Unit 2

Grammar builder

1 Find and circle past tense verbs in the story *The Hare and the Tortoise*. Write them below.

_____

_____

2 Work with your partner. Circle the correct past tense of the verb. Then say the word.

1	smash	smasheed	smashd	smashed
2	play	played	plays	playd
3	kick	kicked	kicked	kicking
4	happen	happened	happens	happened
5	move	moves	movd	moved

3 Listen to your teacher. Then complete the sentences.

1 We _____ all night at the party.

2 Kevin _____ in New York for two years.

3 Mary _____ me to her birthday party.

4 I _____ the teacher if I could go on the

trip to the zoo.

214

Chapter 22

 **Let's write**

1. Work in groups of three or four. Talk about traditional animal stories you know, and choose one to write about. For example: *Anansi*, *River Mumma* or one that you choose as a group.

2. Use the questions to help you write your story.
   - Describe the characters.
   - What happens in the story?
   - How does it end?
   - What is the lesson people can learn from the story?

3. Draw and write the story.

215

Term 2 Unit 2

Chapter 23

Speaking and listening

1. Work with your partner. Kelly is going to make a speech. Look at the pictures. Can you guess what the speech is about?

2. Take turns to read Kelly's speech. Then ask and answer the questions.

> Hello everyone. I am Kelly Brown. I want to talk to you about reusing old things. We often throw away things when we finish with them, but, in my opinion, we can reuse almost anything, for example, plastic bottles. Throwing them away causes waste and pollutes the environment. We can use old plastic bottles for lots of different things like growing plants, storing drinks and other food. We can use glass jars and bottles in the same way. We can use old tins to keep things in or also to grow plants in. Throwing away old car tyres

creates a lot of waste and pollution. Instead, old car tyres can be used as swings. We can also reuse our old clothes to make new clothes or things for the house like cushion covers. So, next time you are about to throw something away, think about what you can reuse it for. Thank you!

1 How does Kelly start her speech?
2 What three words does Kelly use to say what she thinks?
3 What does Kelly say we can do with old plastic bottles?
4 How does Kelly finish the speech?

3 Work in groups to prepare a speech about reusing one of the things shown in the pictures. Use the tips below to help you.

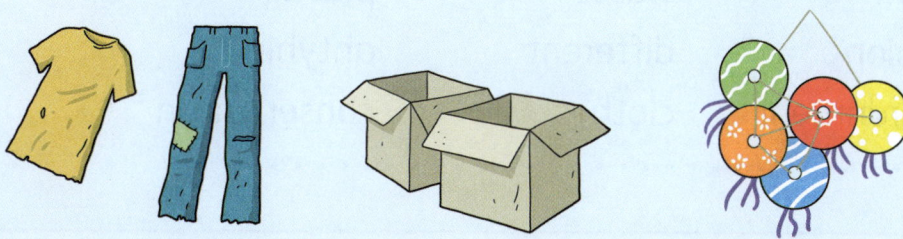

- Start by greeting everyone and introducing yourself.
- Say what your speech is about and what your opinion is.
- Give more detail about the topic.
- Give reasons why you believe in the issue. Give examples.

4 Give your speech to the class. Every member of the group should speak. For example:
- Student A can do the introduction and say what the speech is about.
- Student B can give more details.
- Student C can give reasons and examples.

Word builder

1 Match the syllables to make words.

1	re	a	ion
2	po	b	thing
3	bot	c	use
4	cush	d	llute
5	some	e	tle

Remember ☆☆☆

Words are broken down to parts that each contains one vowel. These parts are called **syllables**. A syllable can be a sound or a beat. Short words may have just one or two syllables, but longer words can have more.

2 Say the words, then put them in the correct list.

Word box

throw	waste	plastic
opinion	different	antyhing
environment	clothes	conservation

One syllable	Two syllables	Three syllables	Four syllables
_____	_____	_____	_____
_____	_____	_____	_____
_____	_____	_____	_____

3 Work with your partner. Student A closes their eyes. Student B chooses a word from Activity 2 and claps the number of syllables it has. For example, Student B will clap 3 times for the word o*pin*ion. Student A must guess the word.

Let's read

Marsha-Lee Hamilton is from Portland in Jamaica. Marsha is just 19 and already becoming famous in her country. Marsha makes dolls from recycled materials. She won third place in the *Jamaica 4-H Clubs Girl of the Year* competition.

Marsha makes male and female dolls from old stockings, wool and old clothes. Even the boxes that she puts her dolls in are made from recycled materials. Marsha has found a creative way to use the items that people usually throw away. She thinks it is important to recycle materials and protect the environment.

When Marsha was young, she always enjoyed making crafts. Marsha also makes teddy bears and some furniture. She gets ideas from watching other artists or from reading craft magazines.

1 Read the text. Are the sentences true (T) or false (F)?
 1 Marsha is 19. _____
 2 Marsha is not very creative. _____
 3 Marsha used old things to make dolls. _____
 4 Marsha won first place in the *Jamaica 4-H Clubs Girl of the Year*. _____
 5 Marsha only makes female dolls. _____
 6 Marsh believes it is important to protect the environment. _____
 7 Marsha has always loved making crafts. _____
 8 Marsha gets inspired from magazines. _____

Grammar builder

L👀k and learn

Some past tense forms of verbs are spelt with a **double consonant**. For example, the past tense of *stop* is *stopped*.

1 Write the past tense of the verbs.

1. happen _____
2. plan _____
3. rob _____
4. travel _____
5. drop _____
6. slip _____
7. knit _____
8. label _____
9. kidnap _____
10. fit _____

2 Complete the text with the past tense of the verbs in brackets.

Last week I went to an art workshop. It ¹_____ (be) great fun. The teacher had lots of old materials. We ²_____ (pick) some materials and then worked on our projects. My project was to make a jewellery box. I ³_____ (paint) a cardboard box blue. Then I ⁴_____ (add) some shells to the cover of the box. I ⁵_____ (sew) them onto the box with pieces of twine. Around the sides of the box I ⁶_____ (paint) fish. I really ⁷_____ (enjoy) doing it and I also made some new friends. I learned that we can reuse old objects for art and crafts.

Let's write

Look and learn
- A **report** tells you information about something.
- Reports have a **title** so the reader knows what it is about.
- The **first sentence** introduces the topic of the report.
- A report is organised into **paragraphs**. The paragraphs can have headings to make it easier for the reader.

1. Work in groups of three or four. You are going to make a school bus using an egg carton box. You will need:

- egg carton
- yellow paint
- paintbrush
- paper
- scissors
- glue
- pieces of old clothes
- bottle caps.

2 Write a report about what you made. Use the past tense. When you finish, check your grammar, spelling and punctuation.

Title: _____

Project:

What was the project?

Why did you do it?

_____

_____

Materials:

What materials did you use?

_____

_____

Results:

What did you make? _____

What did you learn from doing the project?

_____

_____

Chapter 24

Speaking and listening

1 Work in a group. Read how to make a bottle fish.

You will need:
- plastic water bottle
- scissors
- tape
- coloured markers
- glue
- two buttons.

Instructions:
1 Squeeze the bottle in the middle.
2 Cut off the end.
3 Cut triangles into the sides of the bottle.
4 Put tape over the triangle holes.
5 Paint the fish pattern.
6 Glue on the button eye.

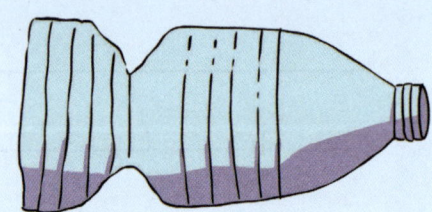

2. Choose one item that your group can make from the following examples, or add your own idea.
   - a pot for growing a plant
   - an old tyre to swing from
   - a toy box
   - your group's idea

   _____

   _____

3. Now draw a poster about what your group plans to make.
   1. Draw and write the materials you must use.
   2. Write about how to make it.

4. Give a presentation to your class and use your poster to help you.

Remember ☆☆☆
- Speak clearly.
- Use the poster to explain what you have to do to make your object.
- At the end, ask if there are any questions from the audience.

Word builder

> **L👀k and learn**
>
> Some words have **silent letters** that we do not pronounce when we say them. Which is the silent letter in the word *talk*?

1 Say the word then colour in the silent letter.

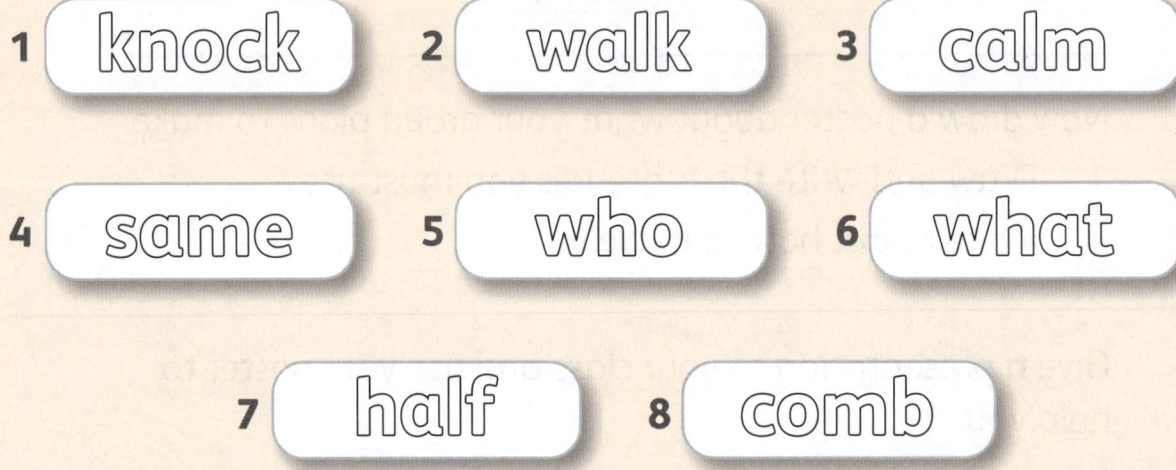

> **L👀k and learn**
>
> There are two ways to spell words with the sound *oi*.
>
> In a one syllable word,
>
> use *oi* in the middle of the word as in *coin*
>
> use *oy* at the end of the word as in *boy*.
>
> In longer words,
>
> use *oy* in the middle of a syllable as in *loyal*
>
> use *oy* at the end of a word as in *annoy*.

2 Sort the *oi* and *oy* words by writing them in the correct box.

oi	oy
coin voice	boy loyal

Word box

toy	boil	enjoy	toilet
soil	coil	royal	point
foil	destroy	cowboy	
joy	moist	noise	

3 Look at the words in your table. Use one colour to underline the words with one syllable. Use another colour to underline the words with more than one syllable. What can you notice?

Let's read

Look and learn

Instructions tell a person how to do something. They need to be short and clear. Drawings can help to make instructions clear to the reader. We use the present tense for instructions.

1. In groups, talk about something you made in Grade 1 or at home in the past; perhaps you made a pot from a used tin, or a toy house made out of cardboard. How did you make it? What did you use it for?

2. Work in groups of three or four. Read the instructions and make the pencil holder.

How to make a pencil holder

You will need:

- cardboard container, for example: a toilet roll or a milk carton
- lollipop sticks
- sticky tape
- glue
- scissors
- paintbrush
- paints
- rubber bands
- coloured paper.

Time: 20 minutes

Chapter 24

Instructions

1. Cut the container until it is the right size to hold pens or pencils. Use one of the lollipop sticks to measure the container and make sure it is cut to the right size.
2. Cut the paper so it is the same size as the container.
3. Glue the paper to the container so it is covered.
4. Glue the lollipop sticks to the container. Make sure you glue them vertically. Make sure the lollipop sticks are evenly spaced so the container can sit flat on a table.
5. Put two elastic bands around the container to hold the lollipop sticks in place while the glue dries.
6. When the glue dries, take off the rubber bands and paint and decorate the lollipop sticks the way you want.
7. Leave the paint to dry.

Grammar builder

Remember ☆ ☆ ☆

The **present continuous** tells us what is happening now. We form the present continuous with the base form of the verb *to be* + verb + *ing*. Look at the table to see how we form a full sentence using the present continuous.

Person	Subject	Base form of the verb *to be*	Verb + *ing*	Object
a single person	I	am	watching	TV.
a single person	You	are	watching	TV.
a single person	He / She / It	is	watching	TV.
More than one person	We	are	watching	TV.
More than one person	You	are	watching	TV.
More than one person	They	are	watching	TV.

Mary is watching TV.

Chapter 24

1 Look at the pictures and complete the sentences with the present continuous form of the verbs in the box.

1 He _____ (wait) at the bus stop.

2 She _____ (talk) on the phone.

3 They _____ (play) football.

4 You _____ (shout). Stop making so much noise!

5 We _____ (do) our school work quietly.

L👀k and learn

Questions that can be answered with *yes* or *no* are formed by changing the order of the subject and the verb and adding a question mark. For example: *You are watching TV.*
Are you watching TV?

231

2 Write questions in the present continuous.

1 you / read / a book?

_____

Yes, I am.

2 Winston / play / in the park?

_____

No, he is not.

3 they / eat / dinner?

_____

Yes, they are.

4 you / work / on the project?

_____

Yes, we are.

Remember ☆☆☆

Do you remember the **past continuous** from Chapter 6? The past continuous tells us what was happening in the past. We form the past continuous with the past form of the verb *to be* + verb + *ing*.

Person	Subject	Past form of the verb *to be*	Verb + *ing*	Object
a single person	I / You / He / She / It	was	watching	TV.
More than one person	We / You / They	were	watching	TV.

Remember

Formation of the past continuous tense

past tense of the verb **be** + verb **-ing form**

He was reading.

3 Write questions in the past continuous.

1 She / read / a book?

<u>Was she reading a book?</u>

Yes, she was.

2 Winston / play / in the park?

_____

Yes, he was.

3 they / eat / dinner at the Caribbean restaurant / yesterday?

_____

Yes, they were.

4 you / work / on the project?

_____

Yes, we were.

Let's write

1. Work in groups of two or three. Think of something you want to make with old materials. For example, something to wear, something to use at school, a toy for your brother or a bag for your sister.

   You will need:

   _____

   _____

   _____

   _____

   _____

2. Write instructions on how to make the object. Remember that instructions should be short and clear. Look at the "Let's read" lesson for help and use the words below if you need them.

   Word box

cut	use scissors to	tie with string
glue	paint	paper
sew	rubber bands	use safety pins to
draw	coloured pencils	
use sticky tape to	cover with	

Chapter 24

Instructions:

| 1 | 2 |

| 3 | 4 |

| 5 | 6 |

235

Term 2 Unit 2 Review and assessment

Speaking and listening

1   Work with your partner. Describe the pictures.

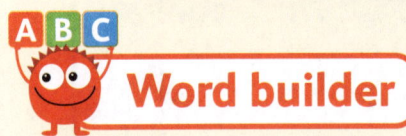
Word builder

1   Look at the pictures. Say the word, then write it.

1 b _____   2 ch _____   3 y _____

 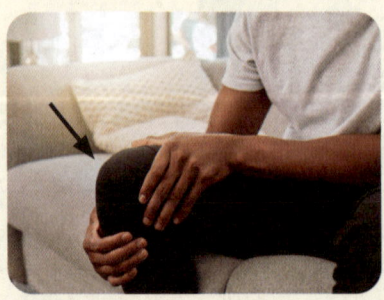 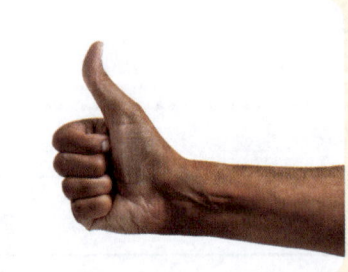

4 c _____   5 kn _____   6 th _____

Review and assessment

Let's read

Read the instructions and make the object.

Feed the birds in your garden with this amazing bird feeder.
You will need:
paper plate
string
cardboard toilet roll
glue
scissors
hole punch
paint.

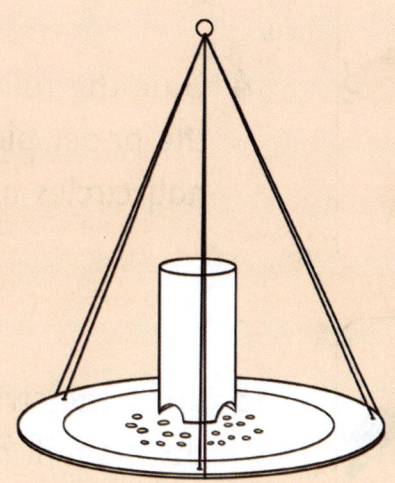

Instructions

1 Paint and decorate the toilet rolls and the paper plate how you want. Leave them to dry.

2 Punch three holes in the paper plate to form a triangle.

237

Term 2 Unit 2

3 At the end of the roll, cut two small half circles on opposite sides.

4 Glue the roll to the centre of the paper plate with the small half circles at the bottom.

5 Loop the string through the three small holes, fill the roll with bird seed and tie to a tree using the string.

6 Watch the birds enjoy their food!

Grammar builder

Remember ☆☆☆

We make a regular noun plural by adding **-s**. For example: *hat – hat**s***.

Irregular plural nouns have different rules which you should learn and remember. For example: *knife – knives*.

1 Make the nouns below plural.

1. box _____boxes_____
2. duck _____
3. cow _____
4. pig _____
5. tomato _____
6. fox _____

Let's write

1. Write a paragraph about the animal and what it does to help people. Think about where they live, what they eat, what they look like and why they are good or how they help people.

> **Example:**
> The pig lives on a farm. It eats grass and vegetables. They are fat and round. We also get pork from pigs. Pigs are good because…

_____

_____

_____

_____

_____

_____

TERM 3

Unit 1

This term will include studying a traditional Jamaican song, learning about advertisements, using mind maps and learning about the weather.

Chapter 25

Speaking and listening

1. Read the song *Jamaica Farewell*.
   Then sing the song with your partner.

   > Down the way where the nights are gay
   > And the sun shines daily on the mountain top
   > I took a trip on a sailing ship
   > And when I reached Jamaica, I made a stop.
   >
   > But I'm sad to say, I'm on my way
   > Won't be back for many a day
   > My heart is down, my head is turning around
   > I had to leave a little girl in Kingston town.
   >
   > Down the market you can hear
   > Ladies cry out while on their heads they bear
   > "Akey" rice, salt fish are nice
   > And the rum is fine any time of year.
   >
   > But I'm sad to say I'm on my way
   > Won't be back for many a day
   > My heart is down, my head is turning around
   > I had to leave a little girl in Kingston town.
   >
   > Sounds of laughter everywhere
   > And the dancing girls sway to and fro

I must declare my heart is there
Though I've been from Maine to Mexico.

But I'm sad to say I'm on my way
Won't be back for many a day
My heart is down, my head is turning around
I had to leave a little girl in Kingston town.

Down the way where the nights are gay
And the sun shines daily on the mountain top
I took a trip on a sailing ship
And when I reached Jamaica I made a stop.

But I'm sad to say, I'm on my way
Won't be back for many a day
My heart is down, my head is turning around
I had to leave a little girl in Kingston town.

Sad to say I'm on my way
Won't be back for many a day
My heart is down, my head is turning around
I had to leave a little girl in Kingston town.

2 Work with your partner. Ask and answer the questions.
   1 What is the song about?
   2 Can you find words that rhyme in the song? Circle them.
   3 What words does the writer use to describe feelings?
   4 How does the song make you feel?
   5 What is your favourite place in Jamaica?
   6 What do you love about it?

Term 3 Unit 1

Word builder

> **L👀k and learn**
>
> When a **vowel** (**a, e, i, o, u**) is followed by an **r**, it changes to a **long vowel sound**.
>
> Say the following words: "fat / far". Can you hear the long vowel sound when *a* is followed by *r*?

1 Practise saying these words. Notice that *e, i* and *u* followed by *r* have the same sound: = er

a	e	i	o	u
car	her	bird	corn	fur

2 Look and say the words. Can you add more words to each box? Look online for more examples of *r-controlled words*.

ar	er	ir	or	ur
calendar	farmer	girl	cord	turtle
_____	_____	_____	_____	_____
_____	_____	_____	_____	_____
_____	_____	_____	_____	_____

242

Chapter 25

3. Use the spelling wheel to make as many words about people ending with the vowel -*er*. Write the words on the line.

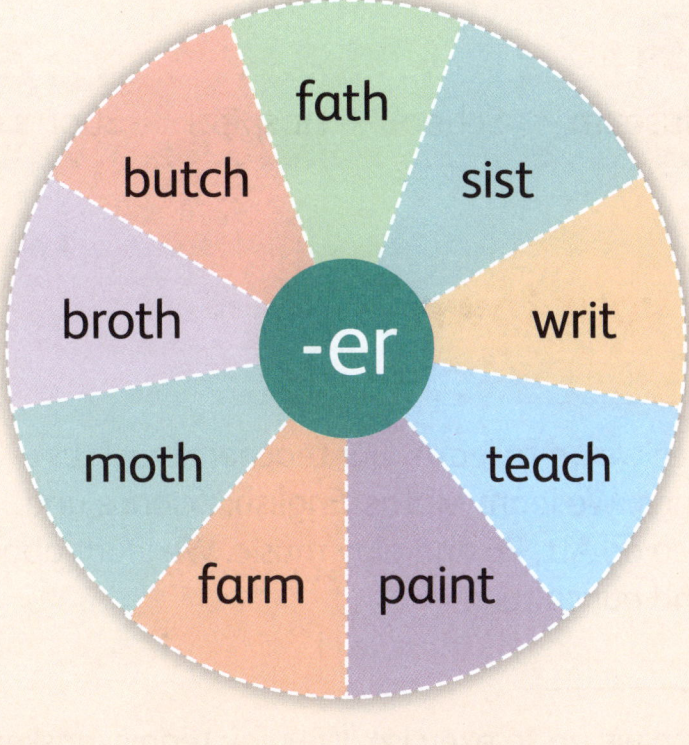

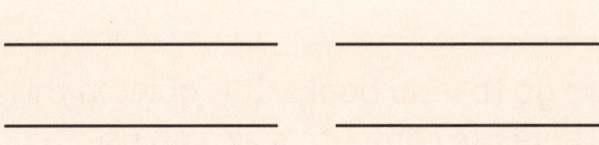

What's your view?
Look at the words ending in -*er*. Can the same person be more than one of these things?

Let's read

1 Choose the correct word for texts 1 to 5 and write them in the space.

Word box

Library   Museum   School   Hospital   Sports centre

Places in your town

1 _____

This is the place we go to learn. Our teachers teach us important things. We learn Maths, English, Science and History. We also do Art, PE and play music. We learn about our country and our culture.

2 _____

This is the place we go to exercise. We play tennis, basketball and football. We can also swim here. There are team games and games we can play on our own. It's a place where we keep fit and stay healthy.

3 _____

This is the place we go to read books. It is quiet in this place so we can study. There are computers we can use to do our homework. We can borrow books from this place. We can also find out information about things. The person who works here is helpful and can tell us where to look for books on different topics.

4 _____

When you have an accident, the ambulance brings you to this place. This is the place we go when we are sick. Doctors and nurses work in this place. They help us to get better. It is usually a big building with lots of different rooms. Some people have to stay here for many weeks until they get better.

5 _____

We sometimes go to this place on school trips. Some of these places teach us about art and history, some teach us about science and there are others that teach us about people. There are paintings, drawings and lots of objects in this place. There are fun workshops for children to teach us things. This place tells us about culture. Administrators work here. Their job is to look after all the exhibitions.

2 Read the texts again and answer the questions.
1 Why do you think teachers are important?
2 Why do people go to the place labelled 2?
3 What can you do in 3?
4 Why is 4 an important place?
5 What can you do in 5?

3 Think about the places in Activity 1 and discuss these questions with your partner.
1 Which of the places have you been to?
2 What did you do in these places?
3 Which of the places do you like best? Say why.
4 Which of the places do you like least? Say why.

Grammar builder

Look and learn
- A **simple sentence** is a group of words with a subject or a plural subject and a main verb.
- The word *and* helps join parts of a subject to make it plural.

For example: Winston and Lloyd go to Alpha primary school.

1 Choose words to make a plural subject with the word *and* to complete the sentence.

Word box

my mother	my brother	my friend
my father	my aunty	I
my sister	my uncle	my family

Example:
My family and I watch the TV programme ER every Friday.

1 _____ and _____ go shopping at the weekend.

2 _____ and _____ play football every evening after school.

3 _____ and _____ wash our hands before having dinner.

4 _____ and _____ already finished our homework at school.

5 _____ and _____ visited my grandparents last weekend.

2 Compare your sentences with your partner.

3 Now write your own sentence and compare with your partner.

4 Match the adjectives to the pictures.

> **L 👀 and learn**
> We use words called **adjectives** to describe people, places and objects. For example, *Anna is **tall***.

1 tall
2 angry
3 noisy
4 cold
5 clean
6 hot

247

Let's write

1. Think of a place you know. Circle the adjectives below which describe it. Can you think of anymore? For example:

   Coronation Market   (noisy)   busy

   Word box

big	quiet	warm	colourful	dirty
noisy	beautiful	clean	pretty	

2. Now write a paragraph about the place. Use the questions below to help you.
   - What is the place?
   - Where is it?
   - What can you do and see there?
   - Who works there?
   - How would you describe it?
   - What do you like about it?

   Example:

   Coronation market is in Kingston. If you go on a Saturday you can see crowds of people buying **delicious** food. The marketers are very **friendly** and people are **helpful**. It is a **big** space and it is very **noisy**. The fruit and vegetables look **beautiful** and **colourful**. In **hot** weather, it can get quite **warm**.

   _____

   _____

   _____

   _____

   _____

Chapter 26

Speaking and listening

1. Work with your partner. Student A is the customer, Student B is the market seller. Role play the conversation.

> **Customer:** How much are the oranges?
>
> **Market seller:** 250 J$ per kilo.
>
> **Customer:** Can I have half a kilo of oranges please?
>
> **Market seller:** Of course. These are the best oranges in all of Kingston! They come from my cousin's farm.
>
> **Customer:** Oh, good. Can I also have some tomatoes, please?
>
> **Market seller:** How many do you want?
>
> **Customer:** Eight of those big ones.
>
> **Market seller:** OK. That is 300 J$. Anything else?
>
> **Customer:** Yes, I will have two onions.
>
> **Market seller:** Is that everything?
>
> **Customer:** Yes.
>
> **Market seller:** Alright, that comes to a total of 650 J$.
>
> **Customer:** Here you are.
>
> **Market seller:** 1000 J$. There is your change. 350.
>
> **Customer:** Thanks. Goodbye.
>
> **Market seller:** Bye!

2 Work with your partner. Use your own ideas to complete the conversation, then role play with your partner.

Market seller: Good morning. Can I help you?

Customer: Good morning. Yes, can I have some ¹_____ .

Market seller: Yes, of course. How many?

Customer: ²_____. How much are they?

Market seller: That is ³_____ .

Customer: Do you have any ⁴_____ ?

Market seller: Yes. How many would you like?

Customer: Can I have ⁵_____, please?

Market seller: Here you are. Would you like anything else?

Customer: No, thanks.

Market seller: OK, that is ⁶_____ .

Customer: Here you are.

Market seller: Thank you.

Word builder

L👀k and learn

Some words are called **voiced** because they make a sound that comes from your throat and the sound makes your throat vibrate. For example, *z* as in *toys*, *boys*.

Some words are called **unvoiced** because they only make a sound in your mouth. For example, *s* as in *bus*, *cats*.

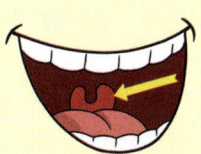

1. The *s* sound makes a hissing sound, like a snake and comes from hissing the air out of your mouth. With your partner, hiss like a snake and take turns to say the followings words: **c**ircle, **s**ad, **s**aid, **s**it.

2. The *z* sound makes a buzzing sound, like a bee and comes from your throat. With your partner, buzz like a bee and take turns to say the followings words: chee**se**, plea**se**, free**ze**, bo**ys**, kne**es**, bab**ies**, dog**s**, cook**ies**, finger**s**, flower**s**, sunri**se**.

3. Work with your partner. Say the words and put them under the correct sound *s* or *z*. Then add your own *s* and *z* words.

Word box

nose	circle	bus
rose	face	boys

251

Term 3 Unit 1

s	z

Remember ☆☆☆

A **syllable** can be a sound or a beat. Short words may have just one or two syllables, but longer words can have more. How many syllables are there in the word market?
Example: mar*ket

4 Count the syllables in these words.

buy _____   kilo _____

customer _____   change _____

bananas _____   potatoes _____

ackee _____   rice _____

tomatoes _____   shopping _____

Let's read

1 Work with your partner. Student A is John. Student B is Clive. Role play the conversation.

John: Hey Clive, how are you?

Clive: I am fine, man. My fruit is doing well.

John: That is good news, Clive. Do you still sell your fruit in the market?

Clive: Yes, I do. I sell mangoes, bananas and pineapples from the farm.

John: How much does it cost to have a stall at Kingston market?

Clive: For a day, it will cost you about 1000 J$.

John: Really? That is expensive.

Clive: Yes, I know. It's really difficult for me to pay that every week, so now I only go there once a month to sell my fruit.

John: I have an idea, Clive. Could we share a stall at the market? We can sell your fruit and my vegetables. I have onions, potatoes, yam and carrots. We can offer the customers more choice. We can each pay 500 J$ for the stall and use it twice a month. What do you think about that?

Clive: Hey – that is a really good idea! We should do it!

2 Read the conversation and answer the questions.

1. Do you think that John and Clive are friends? Explain one way that you know.

   _____

2. Why did John and Clive decide to share a stall at the market?

   _____

Term 3 Unit 1

Grammar builder

Remember ☆☆☆

Pronouns replace nouns. We use pronouns so we do not have to repeat the name of the person, place, thing or idea.

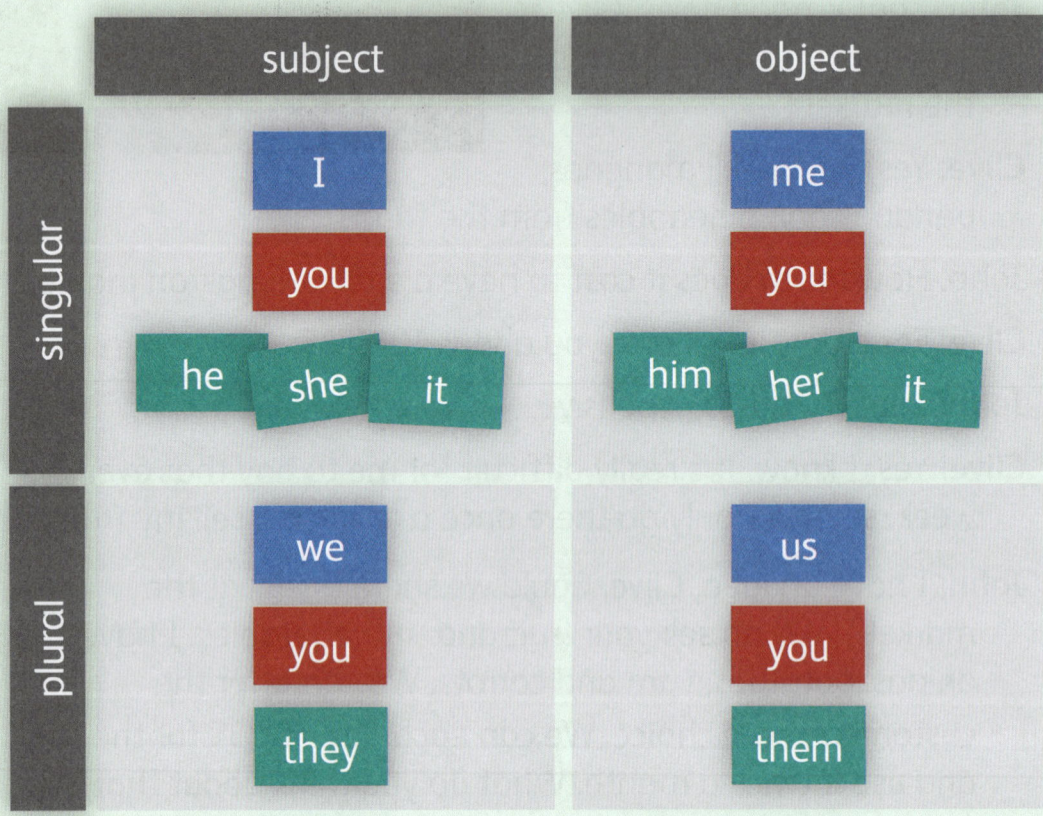

1 Replace the words in brackets with subject pronouns.

1 (Jackie) _____ goes shopping every week at the market.

2 (Phil and I) _____ play basketball on Saturday.

3 (Eric and John) _____ are in my class.

4   (Tom) _____ is a farmer.

5   (The dog) _____ is hungry.

2 Work with your partner. Replace the words in brackets with a pronoun. Then write whether it is a subject pronoun, "S" or an object pronoun, "O".

> **Example:**
> My brother works really hard.
> (My brother) **He** is a fireman. **S**
> The pencils are in the drawer. Can you get (the pencils) **them** please? **O**

1   Alicia is my baby sister. I love (Alicia) _____ . _____

2   Calvin and Dan come from London, but now (Alex and Amy) _____ live in Kingston. _____

3   Alex likes swimming. (Alex) _____ often goes to the beach. _____

4   I have a parrot called Charlie. (Charlie) _____ is four years old. _____

5   That is my Maths teacher, Mr. John. Can you see Mr. (John) _____ ? _____

6   My name is Sarah. (Sarah) _____ am seven years old. _____

> **Remember** ☆ ☆ ☆
> We use words called **adjectives** to describe people, places and objects.
> For example: *Jack is **strong***.

3 Underline the adjectives in the sentences. The first one is done for you.

1 Karen is very <u>tall</u>; she is nearly 2 metres.
2 Eric is strong and he can lift weights.
3 I feel happy when I eat chocolate.
4 Jason is a fast runner and he wins all the races.
5 The old woman sells vegetables at the market.
6 The mouse is small that it can squeeze under the door.

Chapter 26

Let's write

1 Work in groups of two or three. Write a conversation in a market. Use the words and phrases below to help you.

Word box

Can I help you?   Here you are.
How much… ?   Do you have any… ?

Think about:
- what things you want to sell or buy
- how much they cost
- how to make the dialogue interesting.

_____

_____

_____

_____

_____

_____

As a group check your work for neat handwriting and correct punctuation. Also check your maths.

2 Role play your dialogue for the class.

Chapter 27

Speaking and listening

1. Work with your partner. Read the texts. Ask and answer the questions.
   1. What kind of texts are they?
   2. Who do you contact if you want to learn street dance?
   3. Which text is selling an object?
   4. What information in the 2nd text would persuade you to book a piano lesson?
   5. What is the largest group of people Laura will teach?

A Bike for sale 20,000 J$

This fantastic BMX bike is for sale. It's fast and it is in good condition.

Please contact Jimmy on 0135 786 5674

B

Piano Lessons

**Do you want to learn how to play the piano?
Can you already play, but want to improve?**

I am a qualified music teacher with 10 years' experience in teaching music. I am friendly and patient. My lessons are fun and many of my students have gone on to become great musicians.

I teach children and adults.

Call or email Hannah on 816-3357-3836 or hannah1984@googlemail.com

C

Laura's Dance School

We are a small dance school offering classes to groups of up to ten students.

Classes for all levels

Dance classes we offer:

tap   ballet   street dance   modern dance

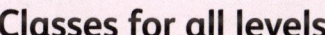

Our teachers have years of teaching experience.
Call 1039-3934-6867 to find out more information and book a place on one of our popular courses.

2. Talk with your partner about an advertisement you have seen. What was it selling? Was it a good advertisement, did it make you want to buy what it was selling?

Word builder

Look and learn

Synonyms are words that have a close meaning. For example: *That milkshake is big.* and *That milkshake is large.* have the same meaning.

1 Colour in the words that are synonyms.

1	small	large	tiny	fast
2	cold	wet	warm	freezing
3	skinny	fat	thin	short
4	difficult	strange	easy	simple
5	delicious	tasty	hot	salty
6	noisy	calm	loud	funny
7	bad	good	rich	horrible

2 Look at the advertisements in the "Speaking and listening" lesson and find three adjectives. Write the adjectives in the table below. Then use a dictionary to find synonyms for those adjectives.

Look and learn

We use words called **adjectives** to describe people, places and objects. For example: *Jamaica is **beautiful**.*

Adjectives	Synonyms
fantastic	amazing

Chapter 27

Let's read

1. Work with your partner. Look at the pictures. What do you think the text is about?

Last weekend, Aaliyah, Corinne and Kevon decided to have a picnic at the beach. The children counted how much money each of them had. Aaliyah had 3000 J$, Corinne had 2350 J$ and Kevon had 1500 J$. They also needed some money for the bus tickets to and from the beach. A return ticket cost 200 J$. They decided to put all their money together and share all the food. This meant they could also buy more things.

The children made a list of things to buy before they went to the supermarket. They decided to get bread to make sandwiches, cooked chicken and some vegetables to make a salad, some mangoes and soft drinks.

After they finished shopping, the children went to the beach to have their picnic. The weather was warm and the sea was beautiful. They made sandwiches and a big salad with all the vegetables they bought. It was really nice.

After eating, the children played games. Then they went for a swim. Late in the afternoon, the children got the bus home. It was a great day! All the children were very happy.

2 Look at the words in the table. Find a synonym for each word in the text and write them below.

hot	pretty	huge	good	super	joyful

3 Read the text. Answer the questions.
1. Who has the most money out of the three children?
2. What do the children decide to do with their money? Why?
3. What did the children buy?
4. Where did they go after the supermarket?
5. What did they do after eating?
6. How did the children feel at the end of the day?

4 Think of a time you shared something with a friend. Tell your partner and ask and answer the questions.
1. How did it make you feel?
2. Do you think it's good to share? Why? Why not?

Chapter 27

Grammar builder

Look and learn
Possessive pronouns show who owns something.
Possessive pronouns can:
- come **before** a noun. For example: *This is **my** toy.*
- **replace** nouns. For example: *Is this Helen's toy? No, it's **mine**.*

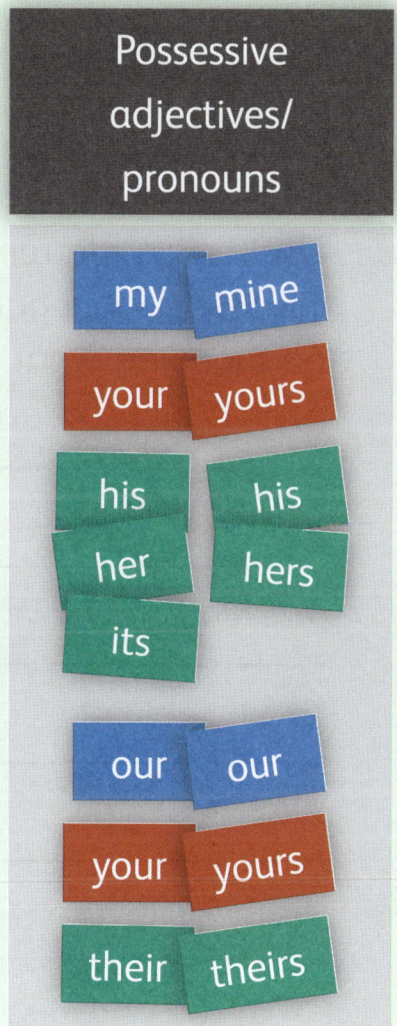

Possessive adjectives/pronouns

my — mine
your — yours
his — his
her — hers
its
our — our
your — yours
their — theirs

1 Change the sentence to show the possessive pronoun coming before the noun.

 1 This is <u>my family's</u> house.

    This is our house.

 2 Where is <u>Winston's</u> hat?

    _____

 3 Here is <u>Anna and Jake's</u> classroom.

    _____

2 Change the sentence to show the possessive pronoun replacing the noun.

 1 The red coat is <u>Jessica's</u>.

    The red coat is hers.

 2 This house is <u>my family's</u>.

    _____

 3 That is <u>my book</u>.

    _____

Let's write

1 Work with a partner and circle the correct pronouns in the letter.

> Hello Grade 2,
>
> My / me name is Jessica. I am a student at Wood Green school in the UK. Our / us teacher said that you are doing a project on shops. Our / us shops in the UK are very nice. Last week I bought me / my mother a gift for she / her birthday. I also bought my / me sister a T-shirt.
>
> Best wishes,
>
> Jessica

2 Use Jessica's letter to help you write a letter back to her. Tell Jessica your name, which school you go to, where you go shopping, what you bought.

_____
_____
_____
_____
_____
_____

Chapter 28

Speaking and listening

1. Read the poem quietly to yourself.

> I live by the river
> It flows like the wind
> It slides and writhes over rocks and stones
> It carries life to the sea
> It sounds like the laughter of children
> It feels as fresh as morning dew.
>
> I live by the river
> It is long and wide like a snake
> It cuts through the forest
> It carries people to different places
> It sounds like peace and calm
> It feels as smooth as silk.

2. Think about the following:
   1. What part did you notice the most?
   2. What did you understand from the words and phrases?
   3. How did you connect with the poem using your memories and feelings?
   4. Now read the poem out loud to your partner, and talk about your responses to the questions.
   5. Does reading the poem out loud make you understand more about the poem?

3 Ask and answer the questions.
   1 Where does the writer live?
   2 Does the writer like living there?
      How do you know?
   3 Do you like or dislike the poem?
      Why / Why not?
   4 Would you like to live along the river?
      Why / Why not?

4 If you could choose to live anywhere in Jamaica, describe where and why you would like to live there.

Word builder

> **Remember** ☆☆☆
> When a **short vowel** (a, e, i, o, u) is followed by an **r**, the **r** changes the sound to a **long vowel** sound.

1. With your partner, practise saying the following words:

a	e	i	o	u
cat / car	bed / her	twin / bird	block / corn	fun / fur

2. Circle the correct ending to spell the word correctly, then say the words.

   1. sail   ir   or
   2. farm   or   er
   3. doct   ar   or
   4. teach   er   ir
   5. flow   ir   er
   6. administrat   or   ar

   Use a computer or dictionary to look up the words. Did you get the spellings correct? Were some words more difficult than others?

3. Look and find the words in the word snake.

robbertigertailorauthorcalendarcarturtlefarmer

4. Make your own word snake with at least five words and ask your partner to find the words.

Let's read

1 Work with your partner. Look at the picture. What do you think the text is about?

St Elizabeth is a quiet area of Jamaica with lots of pretty fishing villages. The largest river in Jamaica, The Black River, flows through this area. St Elizabeth has many beautiful natural places and small fishing villages.

The fishers in these villages build their boats out of cotton trees. They paint their boats in bright colours. These are the same style of boats that the Arawak Indians used many centuries ago. Some of the people today still move from place to place by boat.

Most of the people in the villages are fishers or farmers as there are not many other jobs. The fishers go out early in the morning to look for fish. The farmers grow different crops.

Chapter 28

The women often sell the fish and crops in the markets. Life in the fishing villages is more relaxed than in big cities like Kingston. The people live a simple life and they like it. Things are cheaper than in the city. The people are poorer than some people in cities. They do not have a lot of technology or other modern things. But they are usually quite happy. They like to be so close to nature. They eat healthy food, like fish, goat, vegetables and rice. Often, their families have been farmers and fishers for generations. Sons take over their fathers' fishing boats or farms so as to provide for their families.

Sometimes, life can be hard along the river when there are hurricanes and floods that destroy houses and crops. At other times, when there are very few fish to catch. But generally, life along the river is peaceful and happy.

> **What's your view?**
> Why do you think poor people who do not have a lot of technology or other modern things are happy?

2 Read the text and answer the questions.
   1. Which is the largest river in Jamaica?
   2. What are the boats made of?
   3. Who used similar boats in the past?
   4. What jobs do the women in the villages usually do?
   5. Why do you think people live in fishing villages?
   6. Why do the men usually become fishers or farmers?

Grammar builder

Remember ☆ ☆ ☆

To avoid repeating someone's name or the subject of a sentence, we use a **subject pronoun**. For example: **Harry** (subject) *kicked the ball and* **he** (subject pronoun) *scored a goal*. Pronouns can be subjects (*I, you, he, she, it, we, you, they*) that act. – *He kicked the ball*.

Object pronouns (*me, you, him, her, it, us, you, them*) express that the action is done to the pronoun. – *The ball hit* **me**.

1. Circle the pronouns in each sentence. Write "S" for a subject or "O" for an object pronoun.

   1. I really like bananas. _____
   2. You can sit on this chair. _____
   3. It is in the drawer. _____
   4. John always writes to me. _____
   5. I usually walk to school. _____
   6. The teacher wants us to do extra homework. _____
   7. "Where is the ruler?" "Lloyd broke it". _____
   8. Anita bought you a lovely gift. _____
   9. They played in the park. _____

Remember

We use **adjectives** to describe **nouns** such as people, places and objects. For example: *The river is **cool***.

Look and learn

We use **comparative adjectives** to compare two or more people, places or objects.

For short adjectives, such as *fast* or *tall*, we add **-er** to compare two things. For example: *The red boat is fast**er** than the black one.*

Word box

fast　　long　　cold
tall　　strong　　quiet

2 Complete the sentences with the comparative form of the adjectives in the word box.

1 Jessica is _____ than me. She is 170 cm and I am only 150 cm.

2 Alex is _____ than Mark. Alex can lift very heavy weights.

3 The village is _____ than the city. There are more cars and people in the city.

4 The Rio Minho is _____ than the Black River. The Black River is 73 km and the Rio Minho is 93 km.

5 The weather is _____ in England than in Jamaica.

6 I can run _____ than Philip. I beat him in the 100 m race.

Let's write

1. You are going to write a letter to a friend about the St Elizabeth fishing village. Use the text in the "Let's read" lesson and the information below to help you.

   - Why are you writing to your friend?
     I am writing to tell you about…
   - What was the unit about? *The unit was about…*
   - What jobs do people usually have who live near the river? Why?
   - How do people move to different places?
   - Is life quieter or noisier than in cities?
   - Are things cheaper or more expensive than in cities?
   - Why do you think people like living in fishing villages?
   - How are their lives different from people who live in cities?
   - What do you think of fishing villages or river communities? Would you like to live in one? Why? / Why not?

Chapter 28

Dear _____,

How are you?

_____

_____

_____

_____

_____

_____

_____

_____

Remember ⭐⭐⭐

When you write a letter, you start and finish with a **greeting**.

Best wishes,

_____

2 Compare your letter with your partner's and check each other's work for neat handwriting and correct punctuation.

Chapter 29

Speaking and listening

1. Work with your partner. Talk about the pictures.
2. Take turns to ask and answer one question for each picture.

> **Example:**
> Student A: Where is Montego Bay?
> Student B: It is on the coast.
> Student B: Why is Montego Bay famous?
> Student A: Because people go there for a holiday.

Montego Bay is the second largest city in Jamaica.

Negril Beach is a popular beach.

Falmouth has beautiful buildings.

Ochos Rios is a town in the north of Jamaica.

Some people think Christopher Columbus first landed here.

Old Harbour is a seaside town in the south of Jamaica.

Runaway slaves hid in this place in the past.

People send bananas and coconuts to other countries from Port Antonio.

Word builder

> **Remember** ☆☆☆
>
> **Synonyms** are words that mean exactly or nearly the same as another word. For example, *shut* is a synonym of *close*.

1. Read the text below. Replace the numbered words with the correct synonyms from the word box. Write the words next to the numbers on the next page.

Word box

small	big	still	filled	pretty
~~good~~	hot	quickly	thrilling	sleepy

I had a ¹nice time last weekend. I went to the Negril beach with my friends. The beach is very ²large and ³beautiful. The weather was ⁴warm and sunny.

The sea was ⁵calm so we went swimming. The sea was ⁶full of colourful fish. They swam very ⁷fast and some of them were ⁸tiny. After swimming, we went for a long walk on the beach. There were some boys playing beach volleyball and we asked them if we could join in. They agreed and we played. The game was ⁹exciting. Our team won! After the game we were all very ¹⁰tired so we decided to go home.

1. __good__ 2. _____
3. _____ 4. _____
5. _____ 6. _____
7. _____ 8. _____
9. _____ 10. _____

2 Find and strike through the pairs of synonyms below in the word search.

B	I	G	M	M	D	L	G	W	T
H	K	L	D	E	F	D	N	D	I
G	A	S	L	H	D	I	I	G	N
C	N	L	S	L	I	F	L	F	Y
H	I	I	L	Y	L	U	L	V	A
F	S	A	T	F	Q	U	I	G	P
J	M	T	U	I	V	F	R	O	Q
S	Z	O	I	Q	C	Y	H	O	N
N	I	C	E	L	R	X	T	D	E
F	U	L	L	S	L	F	E	R	B

Word box

~~small / tiny~~
nice / good
calm / still
exciting / thrilling
full / filled

Let's read

1 Read the text. Answer the questions.

> Alicia, Coby and Linda were best friends. One weekend, the three decided to go camping at Discovery Bay. The place is famous because some people believe Christopher Columbus went there, on his way to America. Also, some people think the beach has ghosts so the children were a little scared.
>
> When the children arrived at the beach, they put up their tent near some trees and then went for a swim in the sea. Then, they made a simple lunch of sardines with bread and some oranges. After lunch, they walked along the beach, looking for hidden treasure. Coby believed there was buried treasure there because, a long time ago, a lot of pirates crashed their boats and were shipwrecked on that beach. This is why some people think that there are ghosts in Discovery Bay.
>
> Later that night, the children went to bed. Coby and Linda fell asleep quickly, but Alicia could not sleep. She thought she heard noises outside the tent, then she heard a voice calling out a name. Alicia screamed and the other two children woke up. They all went outside to see if there was someone there.
>
> Suddenly, there was a strange noise near the trees. Coby thought it was probably a small animal, but to help the others feel safe he went to have a look. Linda and Alicia watched as Coby went into the forest. They waited for a few minutes then called to

Coby, but there was no answer. They looked at each other and then went to have a look together. They slowly walked into the forest and searched the area where Coby was. Coby's hat was on the ground, but Coby was not there.

1. Where did the children go camping?
2. Why is the place well known by many people?
3. How did the children feel about the place?
4. What did the children do first when they arrived?
5. Draw what the children had for lunch.

6. What was Coby looking for on the beach?
7. Why could Alicia not go to sleep?
8. What do you think happened to Coby?
9. What do you think Linda and Alicia will do now?
10. Have you ever found any treasure or know anyone that has found something valuable?

Grammar builder

Remember ⭐☆☆

Adjectives can be used to describe places. They make sentences more interesting.

1. Find and circle the adjectives in the text.
2. Complete the sentences with the correct adjectives.

Word box

popular   clean   crowded
famous   sandy   long

1. There is a _____ beach near my home. It is white and sparkles when the sun shines on it.

2. The beach is very _____, there is no litter.

3. Going to the beach is _____ with people at the weekend.

4. Negril Beach is quite _____. It is an 11 kilometre walk.

5. Montego Bay is very _____ with tourists. Lots of people go there on holiday every year.

6. Cave Beach is a _____ beach in Jamaica. Lots of people know it.

Term 3 Unit 1

3 Look at the pictures. Can you think of two adjectives to describe each place?

_____   _____

_____   _____

_____   _____

_____   _____

280

Let's write

1. Work in groups of two or three. Ask and answer the questions.
   1. What can you see?
   2. Do you think people like to go there? Why? Why not?

2. Think of four adjectives to describe the place. Write them in the box.

   ┌─────────────────────────────────────┐
   │   │
   │   │
   │   │
   │   │
   └─────────────────────────────────────┘

3. Write about the place in the picture. Use adjectives to make your description more interesting. Use the information below to help you.

   It is a _____. There are _____.

   The _____ is _____. There is a _____. I like / do not like it because _____.

4 Write about another place of your choice. Remember to use adjectives.

_____

_____

_____

_____

_____

_____

5 Check your spelling and punctuation. Have you started your sentences with a capital letter? Have you used commas and full stops?

Compare your work with your partner.

Chapter 30

Speaking and listening

1. Work with your partner. Look at the pictures and take turns to ask and answer the question.

   What can you see?
   The farmer **is** prepar**ing** the soil.

   Remember ☆☆☆

   You can use the **present continuous** to describe events that are happening in front of you. For example: *The farmer **is** prepar**ing** the soil. The ox is pulling the plough.*

The farmer / prepares / soil.

He / plants / the banana plants.

He / picks / the bananas.

He / puts / the fruit in his truck.

He / sells / his fruit to shops.

People / enjoy / his bananas.

2. Work with your partner. Take turns to describe events that are happening in front of you.

   Example:
   Anna **is** writ**ing**. The teacher **is** clean**ing** the board.

Term 3 Unit 1

Word builder

L👀k and learn

Antonyms are words that mean the opposite. For example, the antonym for *big* is *small*.

1. Colour the antonyms in the same colour.

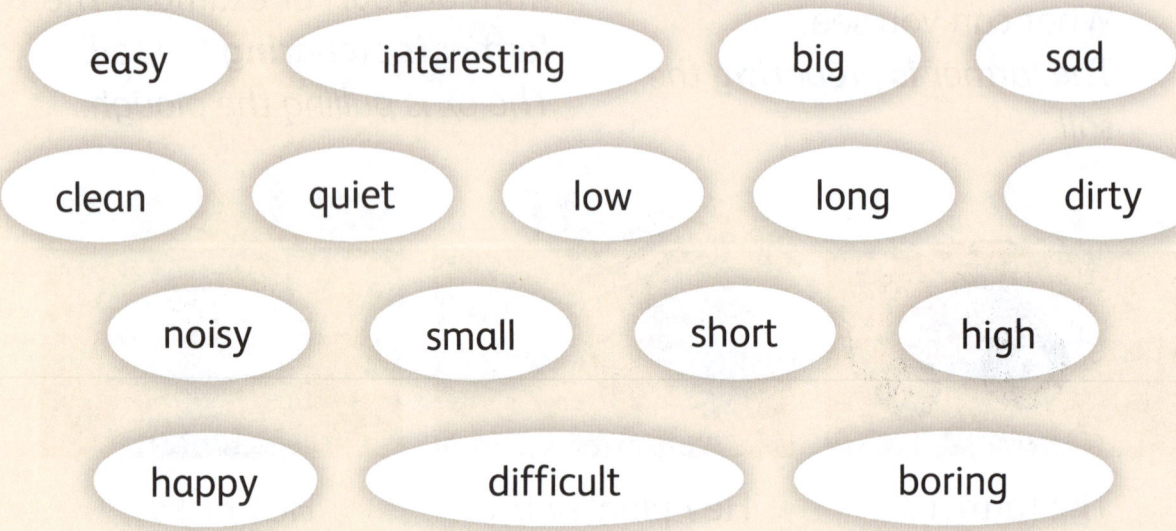

L👀k and learn

When a vowel (**a**, **e**, **i**, **o**, **u**) is followed by the letter **r**, **r** becomes the boss.

Say "cat". Now add the letter *r* after the *a* and say the new word "cart" aloud.

What happens to the *a* sound when you add *r*? The *r* sound is strong and becomes the boss!

2 Look at the posters below. In pairs or small groups, make your own poster, but include a word for *each vowel + r (ar, er, ir, or, ur)*. Write the title of the poster as **"a, e, i, o, u + the Bossy R"**.

Let's read

1. Work with your partner. Ask and answer the question.

   Do you think life on a farm is easy or difficult? Why?

Once, there was a farmer called Mr Jones. He farmed sugar cane. Mr Jones worked hard. He woke up every day at 4 a.m. and worked until the sun went down. He had one son called Lucas. Lucas worked in the sugar cane fields helping Mr Jones to cut the sugar cane.

Mr Jones was well known in his village. He was a friendly man and always helped others. On Saturday mornings, Mr Jones and his wife Rosie sold their sugar cane in the market. Mr and Mrs Jones were very happy with their life on the farm.

Then one year, something terrible happened. Mr Jones' well dried up. He had no water. He had to get water at a river that was five kilometres away. Mr Jones' old donkey was too weak to carry much water. Some of the sugar cane started to die. Mr Jones, Rosie and Lucas ran back and forward from the river in the hot sun carrying buckets of water to the sugar cane fields, but it was no use. They needed more people, but Mr Jones was a proud man and he did not like asking for help.

Then one day, Mr Henry, another farmer was on his way to the market. He saw Mr Jones running with a bucket of water. Mr Henry was surprised how terrible Mr Jones looked. He was thin and looked really hot and tired, so did Rosie and Lucas. He asked them what happened. Mr Henry was sad to hear of their trouble and said goodbye.

Some hours later, a number of people started to arrive at Mr Jones' farm. They had come to help. Everyone in the village was there. They brought donkeys and trucks and they all started carrying buckets of water to the sugar cane fields. They helped Mr Jones find a new well with plenty of fresh water.

2 Read the text and put the pictures in order.
Write the number in the box.

3 Read the text and answer the questions.

1 Why do you think the writer says the farmer worked hard?
   _____

2 How did the villagers feel about the farmer?
   _____

3 What problem did the farmer have?
   _____

4 What do you think Mr Henry did?
   _____

5 What do you think the theme of the story is?
   _____

Grammar builder

Lk and learn

Possessive pronouns show who owns something. They replace the names of people and objects (nouns) in sentences. They can be singular or plural.

For **plural possessive pronouns** we replace the noun with **ours**, **yours**, **theirs**. For example:

Subject · Subject
My neighbour's car is green and my family's car is black.
 · **ours**

1 Complete the sentences with the correct possessive pronouns (*ours*, *theirs*, *yours*). Notice that *ours*, *theirs*, *yours* are at the end of the sentences.

1 Those books belong to us. They are _____.

2 The CDs are Matt and Luke's. They are _____.

3 "Is this phone _____?" "No it is not mine."

4 "Are these socks _____?" "Yes, they are yours."

5 Those shoes are Kelly and Julie's. They are _____.

6 "Is this jacket _____?" "Yes, it is Anna's."

2 Replace the noun that is underlined with a possessive pronoun (*ours*, *theirs*, *yours*). Notice that *ours*, *theirs*, *yours* are at the beginning of the sentences.

1 My family's car is black and <u>my neighbours' car</u> is green.

   Theirs is green.

2   Anna's class starts at 9:00 am. <u>Jane's and my class</u> starts at 10:00am.

    _____

3   Our class' school trip is today. <u>Your class'</u> school trip is tomorrow.

    _____

4   My house is small, but my friends <u>Lucy and Tom's house</u> is large.

    _____

5   Our exam is today. <u>Your class'</u> exam is tomorrow.

    _____

3 Complete the gap with an adjective that fits the context of the sentence.

1   Jessica has five brothers and five sisters. She lives in a _____ house.

2   Angela never speaks to anyone, she is a _____ girl.

3   My school has five floors, it is _____.

4   We have played football all day. We are _____.

5   It is nearly lunch time. I am really _____.

Term 3 Unit 1

Let's write

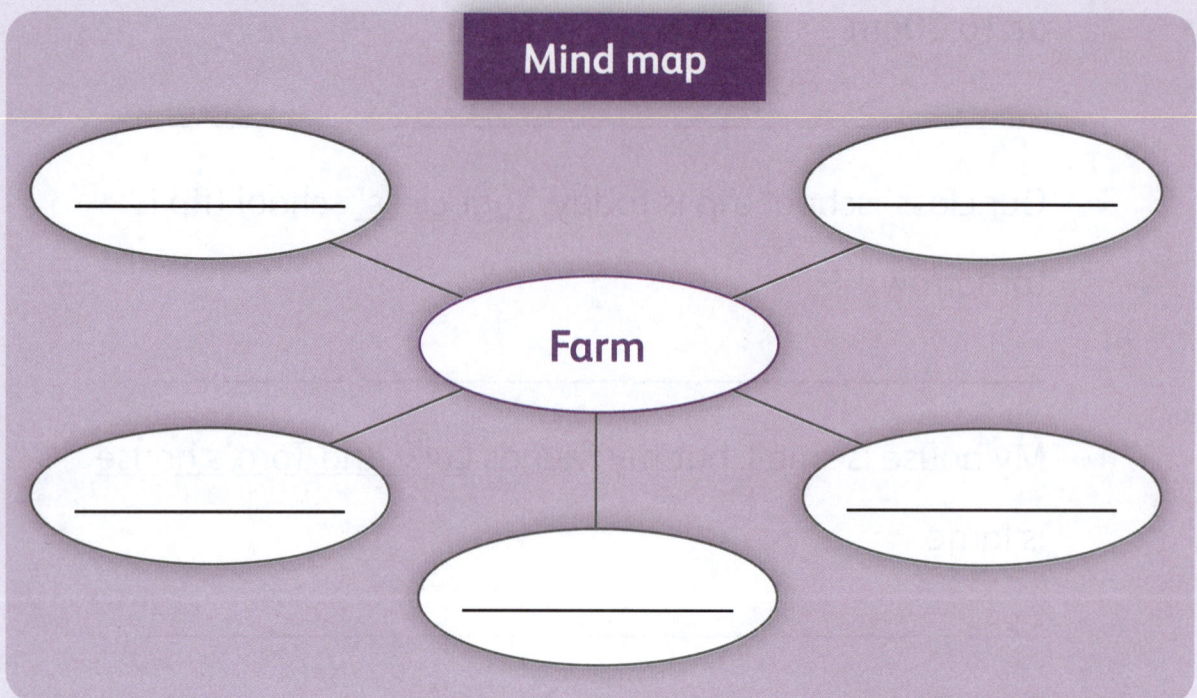

1   Work in groups of two or three. Complete the mind map about activities on a pineapple farm. Use the internet to help you. Ask your teacher to check your mind map when you finish.

2   Choose one of the activities from the mind map and draw it.

3   Write a paragraph about the activity. Use the questions. Do not forget to use adjectives to make your writing more interesting.
    - What is the activity?
    - Who does it?
    - When do they do it?
    - Why do they do it?
    - What happens?

    _____

    _____

    _____

    _____

    _____

4   When you finish, exchange your work with another student and check each other's spelling, grammar and punctuation.

Chapter 31

Speaking and listening

1. Work with your partner. Take turns to read aloud the story.

The Princess and the Pea
by Hans Christian Andersen

Once upon a time, a prince was looking for a true princess to be his wife, but all the princesses he met were not real princesses. The prince was sad.

Many young ladies presented themselves as princesses to the prince, but they were either greedy or unkind. There was always something not right. The queen decided to test the princesses. She put a pea under a pile of mattresses to see if the princesses would feel it when they go to bed. Only a real princess would notice a small pea. They all failed the test and had to leave the palace.

One evening, another young lady came to the palace and said she was a princess. She was dressed in simple clothes and did not look like a princess. So, the queen put her to the test. In the morning the queen asked "How did you sleep?" The princess said "I am so sorry, but I felt something hard and I found a pea in the bed. I just could not sleep."

So, the princess passed the test, because only a real princess would feel a tiny pea under a huge pile of mattresses.

2. Now cover the text and use the pictures to retell the story.

3. Talk together and predict what could happen after the last picture in the story.
4. Take turns to role play a scene of the story with your partner.

Word builder

> **Remember** ☆☆☆
>
> **Synonyms** are words that have almost the same meaning. For example: *That elephant is **large**. That elephant is **huge**.*

1 Can you think of synonyms for the underlined words? Write them on the lines.

1. My bedroom is quite <u>big</u>. It can fit two beds, a desk, a chair, a wardrobe and two chests of drawers.

   _____

2. The book is very <u>slim</u>, it only has twenty pages.

   _____

3. The waterfall was <u>beautiful</u>. I really enjoyed seeing it.

   _____

4. We had a <u>nice</u> time at the beach. _____

5. The children were <u>tired</u> after the trip to the rainforest.

   _____

6. Jake is very <u>clever</u>, so he always gets good marks at school. _____

7 Helen was <u>sad</u> because she did not pass her test.

_____

8 I am <u>afraid</u> of spiders; I do not like them.

_____

> **Remember** ☆☆☆
>
> **Antonyms** are words that have the opposite meanings. For example: *I **love** vegetables. I **hate** vegetables.*

2 Write an antonym for the word in each balloon.

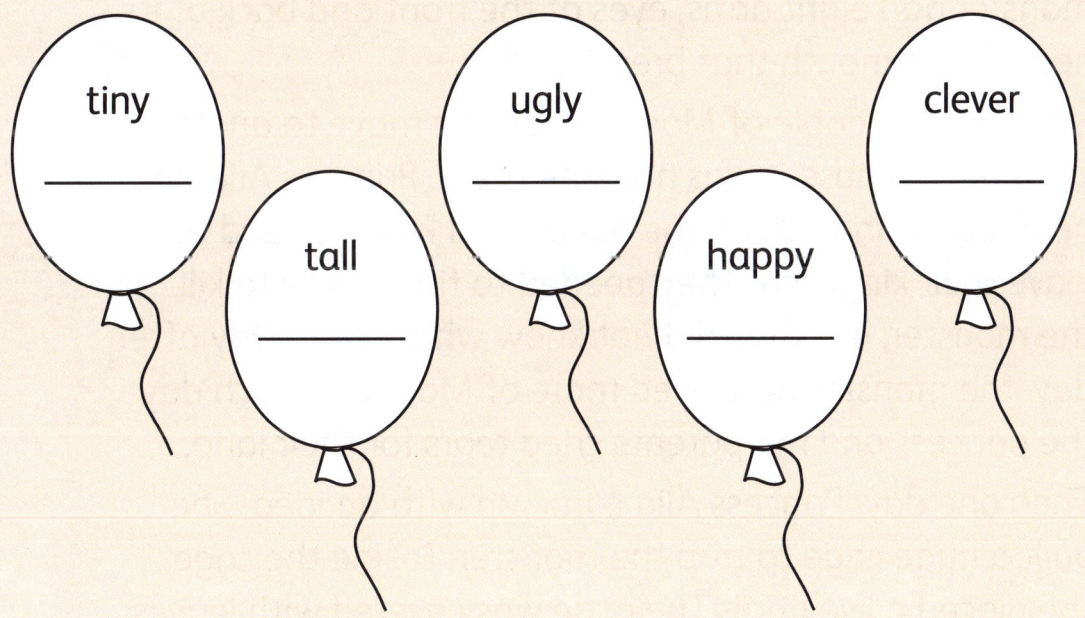

Let's read

1 After you have read the story, ask and answer the questions with your partner.

1. Where does the story take place?
2. Is this place real or imaginary (not real)? How do you know?

Princess Alia lives in the kingdom of Moor. Moor is an island in the sea. It was once a beautiful kingdom with green valleys, thick rainforests and beautiful cities. There were lots of amazing animals in Moor. There were lions with two heads, giraffes the colour of gold and colourful birds that could talk. There were horses that could fly and sheep that could sing. In the past, people came from all over the world to visit Moor. But that was many years ago, before an evil monster attacked Moor. The monster attacked the animals and destroyed the rainforests. The monster had eight arms, eyes at the front and back of its head and a mouth that breathed fire.

Most of the people of Moor decided to move to another kingdom because it was not safe there. Princess Alia and her mother and father, the queen and king, refused to leave their kingdom. They needed to find a way to kill the monster, but they did not know what to do. Day after day, the monster destroyed more of Moor and each day the princess and her parents cried tears for their land.

Then one day, Princess Alia came up with an idea. She built a huge cage to trap the monster. Inside the cage she placed a live goat. The cage was covered with leaves and flowers and placed in the forest near where the Monster lived. The monster looked at the goat and slowly entered the cage. The door now shut with a bang. Once the monster realised it was trapped, it started to roar and throw its enormous body against the sides of the cage. The princess was not afraid. She took out her bow and arrow and killed the monster.

When the people around the world heard the monster of Moor was dead, they came back. Once again, Moor was a happy place to live. News spread about the brave princess and princes came from far to ask her to marry them. The princess chose the bravest prince. So, Princess Alia and her prince were married in the castle and the whole kingdom came to celebrate.

2. Tell your partner about some stories you know that take place in imaginary places.

3. Then tell your partner how you would finish the story flowchart.

L👀k and learn

A **story flowchart** is a drawing of boxes with information and arrows to show the order of when something happens. For example, look at part of the Cinderella story.

| **Cinderella** lived happily with her mother and father until her mother died. | → | **Cinderella's** father married a mean woman who had two daughters. | → | When her father died, **Cinderella's** horrible stepmother turned her into a servant in her own house. |

Term 3 Unit 1

4   Work with your partner. Read the story about the kingdom of Moor again and use your own words to complete the story flowchart.

| The kingdom of Moor was _____ | → | The monster _____ | → |

| The people of Moor moved _____ | → | Princess Alia trapped _____ | → |

| Princess Alia killed _____ | → | The people returned to _____ | → |

Princess Alia and her prince _____

What's your view?
What do you think the theme of this story is?

298

Grammar builder

Look and learn

We use **adjectives** to describe people, places and objects. For example: *Jenny is **nice***.

1 Complete the sentences with the adjectives in the word box.

Word box

short   beautiful   sad   tall
shiny   large   happy   scary

1 The ring is very _____.

2 Karen was _____ because it was her birthday and she got lots of presents.

3 The movie was _____, so people screamed several times in the cinema.

4 The dog is so _____ that it looks like a small horse.

5 Giraffes are very _____, so they can reach up and eat leaves on high trees.

6 Our house is only 10 metres from the beach, so it is a _____ walk.

7 The bird was covered in _____ feathers of every colour.

8 I felt _____ yesterday because my team did not win the match.

299

Let's write

1 Work in groups of two or three. Write a fantasy story. First, use the story flowchart to plan your writing. For example, write about finding a happy farmer who finds some magic beans.

```
┌──────────────┐      ┌──────────────┐
│ _____ │  →   │ _____ │  →
│ _____ │      │ _____ │
│ _____ │      │ _____ │
└──────────────┘      └──────────────┘

         ┌──────────────┐      ┌──────────────┐
         │ _____ │  →   │ _____ │
         │ _____ │      │ _____ │
         │ _____ │      │ _____ │
         └──────────────┘      └──────────────┘
```

_____

_____

_____

_____

_____

2 When you finish, read your work again. As a group, check your spelling, grammar and punctuation.

Chapter 32

Speaking and listening

1. Work with a partner. Take turns to read aloud the weather report.

> The weather on Monday in Kingston will be cloudy and wet in the morning. Remember to take your umbrella when you go out, there will be lots of thunderstorms. Watch out for rainbows in the afternoon as the Sun shines through the rain in some places. It will be a bit windy at times during these thunder storms. Temperatures will reach highs of 33 degrees C and lows of 25 degrees C.
>
> Tuesday will be very much the same with thunderstorms and wind. The temperatures will be similar, with highs of 32 – and lows of 26 degrees. On Wednesday, there will be a sudden change as temperatures drop to 28 degrees and strong winds blow in from the west. There will be a lot of rain with some risk of flooding on Wednesday afternoon and Thursday.
>
> The storms will clear by Friday morning and you will wake up to clear blue skies and sunshine again – a perfect start for the weekend.

Monday	Tuesday	Wednesday	Thursday	Friday
33°C	32°C	28°C	30°C	35°C
25°C	26°C	24°C	26°C	28°C

2   Work with your partner. Look at the chart and talk about what the symbols and numbers mean.

Example:

Student A: On Monday the symbol 🌩 shows rain and lightning.

Student B: Yes, but the weather will still be hot at 33°C.

3   Listen to the weather report again and circle "True" if you think the information is correct or "False" if the information is not correct.

1   You will not need an umbrella on Monday.   True / False

2   On Tuesday the weather will be similar

    to Monday.   True / False

3   There will be flooding only on Thursday.   True / False

4   There will be a storm on Friday.   True / False

Chapter 32

Word builder

1 Sight words

Look at the sight words. Copy each one out in the grid. Cover up the columns and try and write the word in the last column from memory.

crum**ble**	crumble	crumble	
ta**ble**			
sylla**ble**			
un**cle**			
cir**cle**			
cy**cle**			
can**dle**			
nee**dle**			
mid**dle**			

303

2 Find and circle the weather words in the word search.

Word box

rainbow	thermometer	tornado
lightning	hurricane	windy
fog	thunder	

v	y	g	r	a	i	n	b	o	w
h	p	t	o	r	n	a	d	o	r
l	i	g	h	t	n	i	n	g	e
y	d	n	i	w	f	w	a	l	d
r	b	i	c	h	o	s	g	g	n
m	m	e	y	e	g	k	p	d	u
e	n	a	c	i	r	r	u	h	h
m	y	x	x	j	z	s	s	k	t
s	h	e	w	b	e	w	b	z	f
m	x	n	v	i	s	k	h	s	k

Chapter 32

Let's read

1 Read the weather forecast and answer the questions.

5-day forecast for next week

Monday	Tuesday	Wednesday	Thursday	Friday
☀️	⛅	⛈️	🌥️💨	🌪️🌧️
35°C	31°C	31°C	31°C	25°C
27°C	24°C	27°C	25°C	22°C

Monday will be a hot and sunny day. The sea will be calm, so it will be a great day for swimming. The temperature will drop slightly on Tuesday and there will be more clouds in the sky. By Wednesday, there will be thunderstorms with lots of lightning and thunder. Thursday will be cloudy and windy with no rain. It will be a great day for wind surfing! Friday will be a wet and very windy day and temperatures will go down, especially at night. There will be several small tornadoes off the coast of Kingston, so watch out for them.

1. Which day will be good for a trip to the beach?
2. Which days do you need to take an umbrella with you?
3. Which days are good for walking to school?
4. Which day do you need to be careful of strong winds?
5. Which day would be good for flying your kite?
6. Which evening should you wear a jacket when you go out?

Grammar builder

1 Use the present tense of the verbs in brackets to complete the story.

Cleo ¹_____ (be) Mike's pet dog.

She ²_____ (be) in his room. In the morning Mike ³_____ (have) breakfast.

Cleo ⁴_____ (sit) under the table.

Cleo and Mike ⁵_____ (go) for a short walk after breakfast.

After their walk Cleo and Mike ⁶_____ (play) with Mike's ball.

Mike ⁷_____ (kick) the ball and Cleo ⁸_____ (run) after it. Cleo ⁹_____ (love) playing ball with Mike. They both ¹⁰_____ (love) spending time together.

Chapter 32

2 Work with your partner. Complete the sentences. Choose two nouns from the word box to join with *and*. Remember to add a capital letter to the first word in each sentence.

Word box

~~boys girls~~   eggs toast   shoes socks
cheese tomato   milk cookies   fish chips

Example:
The **boys and girls** are working together on their projects.

1. _____ and _____ are good in a sandwich.

2. _____ and _____ are what we have to wear at school. We are not allowed to wear trainers.

3. _____ and _____ are my favourite things to eat for breakfast.

4. _____ and _____ are a nice snack after school.

5. _____ and _____ are served at school for lunch every Friday.

307

Term 3 Unit 1

Let's write

1. Work with your partner. Find out the weather forecast in your town for today. Use the internet.

2. Draw a picture of the weather today.

3. Work in groups of two or three. Write three questions to ask other groups about the weather.

Example:

Is it raining in Jamaica today?

1 _____

2 _____

3 _____

4 Describe the weather today. Use some of the words in the word box and the questions to help you.

Word box

stormy	rainy	thunder
sunny	wet	lightning
cloudy	dry	

- What is the weather like? *Today the sun is shining…*
- What do you think the temperature is? *It is very hot, so I think the temperature is about 35°C.*
- What activities can you do today? *When the weather is hot, we go swimming.*

_____

_____

_____

_____

_____

Chapter 33

 **Speaking and listening**

1. Work with your partner. Partner A is Ann. Partner B is Isaac. Role play the conversation.

Ann: How was the school trip to Ocho Rios?

Isaac: It was fantastic. I really enjoyed it. I am sorry you couldn't go, Ann. How is your leg?

Ann: It still hurts a lot. I was sad that I could not go on the trip. Staying at home all day is boring. Anyway, tell me about it.

Isaac: Of course. Here look, I can show you some pictures. This is the waterfall we went swimming in. The water was so cool and fresh. I felt so good when I jumped in because it was a really hot day.

Ann: Oh, nice. Swimming always makes me feel happy.

Isaac: We also walked in the rainforest. We went every day early in the morning because that is when the animals come out. I was scared because I saw a huge snake wrapped around a tree! There were lots of colourful birds in the trees.

Ann: Oh, I like snakes. My brother has a pet snake. It sounds like a great trip.

Isaac: It was. Do not worry, Ann, you will go on the trip next year.

2. With your partner, take turns to ask and answer the questions.
   1. Where did Isaac go on the school trip?
   2. Why did Ann not go?
   3. How would you feel if you could not go on a school trip because you were sick?
   4. How did Isaac feel about the trip?
   5. How does Isaac feel about snakes?
   6. Why do you think Isaac tells Ann not to worry and that she would go on the trip next year?
   7. Think of a time you felt happy. Where were you? What happened? Who were you with? What did you do?

Word builder

1 Look and say the words.

2 Unscramble the words. Write the correct spelling for each one.

 1 ybo _____

 2 ehlo _____

 3 yto _____

4 tah _____

5 yhpap _____

6 das _____

Let's read

L👀k and learn

A **diary** is written every day and is used to write about what you think, feel, did or need to remember.

Example:

What you did— "I had a great time on the school trip at the museum."

What you need to remember— "On Tuesday afternoon, I have a spelling test!"

Helen Brown's Diary

Dear Diary,

Thursday, 15 April 2021

Today was a fun day at school. I feel happy. We did a project and a presentation. Four of us worked on the project. Our project was about how to reuse things. First, we talked about what to do. Sometimes I felt shy to say my ideas because one of the others was very bossy and loud. His name is Johnny, but then Vicky asked me my opinion and I felt more confident to speak up.

Alex had a really clever idea about using plastic bottles to make houses for people who do not have homes. We made a poster about recycling. Each person worked on a part of the poster. I did the part about paper and cardboard. I used the internet to find out information and then I wrote a paragraph about recycling paper and card. I also drew a picture on the poster.

It was lots of fun working together and sharing ideas. When we finished the poster we prepared a presentation. We decided each person would speak for a few minutes about one thing on the poster. I was really nervous at first when it was my turn to speak, but after a while I felt better. The time went really fast and before I knew it, the presentation was over. Our teacher said we all did a great job and gave us an A+.

1. Read the diary entry and answer the questions.
   1. How did Helen feel about her day?
   2. What did she do?
   3. Who made Helen feel uncomfortable?
   4. What did Vicky do to make Helen feel better?
   5. What was Alex's idea?
   6. How does Helen feel about doing presentations?
   7. What do you think the theme of the diary entry is?
   8. How do you feel about working with others?

Grammar builder

> **Remember** ☆ ☆ ☆
>
> **Possessive pronouns** show who owns something.
> Possessive pronouns can be the object of the sentence:
> *mine, yours, hers, his, ours, yours, theirs.*
> **Example:** *I like your picture. Do you like **mine**?* (object = *my picture*).

1 Complete the sentences with the correct possessive pronouns.

1. This hat is _____. It belongs to me.

2. That house is _____. We live there.

3. That is Jake's bike. It's _____.

4. That cat is _____. It belongs to Victoria and Adam.

5. "Are these apples _____?" "Yes, they are mine."

6. "Are those books _____?" "No they are not Julie's. They are Luke's."

7. I do not like this family's car, but I like _____.

2 Rewrite the sentences using possessive pronouns.

> **Example:**
> Please give Tom this book. **It is Tom's.**
> Please give Tom this book. **It is his.**

1 Those skateboards are <u>Errol and Mark's</u>.

   _____

2 That banana belongs to <u>me</u>.

   That banana is _____.

3 Is that car <u>Adam's</u>?

   _____?

4 That is <u>Peter's</u> computer.

   _____

5 Do those flowers belong to <u>you</u>?

   Are those flowers _____?

3 Work with your partner. Write two sentences of your own using possessive pronouns. Check your sentences with another pair of students. Ask your teacher to check your work when you finish.

_____

_____

Let's write

1. Work with your partner. Ask and answer the questions.
   1. What does a diary page look like? What information is on the page before you use it?
   2. Why do you think people keep diaries?
   3. What tense does the writer use in the text *Helen Brown's Diary* in the "Let's read" lesson?
   4. Do you keep a diary? Why? Why not?

2. Write a diary entry for today. Do not forget to use personal pronouns. Use the questions below. You can include drawings in your diary.
   - What is the date?
   - What happened today (think about things you did at school or at home)?
   - Who were you with?
   - How did it make you feel?

   _____

   _____

   _____

Term 3 Unit 1 Review and assessment 1

Speaking and listening

1. Work with your partner. Ask and answer the questions about the below song.
   1. What is this song? If you do not know, ask your teacher.
   2. What does the word "guard" mean in the second line?
      a control us   b bless us   c protect us
   3. What does the word "grant" mean in the sixth line?
      a give us   b call us   c help us

2. Now stand up and sing the first verse of the national anthem with your partner or together with the whole class.

> Eternal Father bless our land
> **Guard** us with Thy mighty hand
> Keep us free from evil powers
> Be our light through countless hours
> To our leaders, Great Defender,
> **Grant** true wisdom from above
> Justice, truth be ours forever
> Jamaica, land we love
> Jamaica, Jamaica, Jamaica, land we love.

Review and assessment 1

Word builder

> **L👀k and learn**
>
> **Synonyms** are words that have a similar meaning. For example: *That is a **big** dog. That dog is **huge**.*

1 Circle the words that are synonyms.

1	small	large	tiny
2	cold	wet	freezing
3	skinny	fat	thin
4	difficult	easy	simple
5	delicious	tasty	hot
6	noisy	calm	loud
7	bad	good	horrible

Let's read

1 Work with a partner. Tell your partner what you know about farms. What plants and animals can you see on a farm?

2 Read the text on next page. Write true (T) if the sentence is correct or false (F) if it is incorrect.

1. Joshua bought Shaun when he was a baby. _____

2. Shaun was a race horse when he was a foal. _____

3. Joshua knew that his father would miss Shaun. _____

This is a story about Shaun the race horse, a little boy called Joshua and his father. They all lived on an animal farm near Little Orchard. Joshua's dad bought Shaun when he was a baby foal and trained him to race. Joshua's dad needed extra money for the farm. So, he sold Shaun to a neighbour. Joshua's father felt guilty that he had to sell the horse, because he knew that Shaun would miss him.

Joshua cried for many days after Shaun left, so Joshua's father bought Shaun back to the farm. Then a few weeks later, Joshua noticed his father was not eating very much and was very thin. He asked his father what was wrong. His father said that Joshua should not worry.

That evening, Joshua's family had goat curry for dinner, but Joshua saw that his father only had rice on his plate. After dinner he asked his mother why his father was so thin. She said that they did not have enough money for food so Joshua's father would only eat rice.

Joshua was so sad, the next day he decided to ask the neighbour to buy Shaun from his father. The neighbour said he would and told Joshua he could visit Shaun any time. Joshua was happy. He learned that sometimes people must do what is best for everyone.

3 Read the text again and answer the questions.
1 How did Joshua's dad feel when he sold Shaun?
2 What did Joshua do when Shaun left?
3 Why was Joshua's father thin?
4 What decision did Joshua make?
5 What did Joshua learn?

Review and assessment 1

Grammar builder

Look and learn

Possessive pronouns are used to show who owns something. There are two kinds of possessive pronouns:

- Possessive pronouns that come before a noun (*my, your, her, his, our, their, its*). For example: *This book belongs to me. This is* **my** *book.*
- Possessive pronouns that replace nouns (*mine, yours, hers, his, ours, theirs*). For example: *Is this Bob's toy? Is this* **his** *toy?*

1 Replace the underlined nouns to show how the possessive pronoun comes before the noun.

1. This is <u>the family's</u> car. This is _____ car.

2. Where is <u>Anna's</u> book? Where is _____ book?

3. Here is <u>Daniel and Jake's</u> house. Here is _____ house.

2 Replace the underlined nouns to show how the possessive pronoun replaces the noun.

1. The green car is <u>Jessica's</u>. The green car is _____.

2. This house is <u>my family's</u>. This house is _____.

3. That is <u>my book</u>. That is _____.

3 Complete the gaps with a possessive pronoun.

1 My mother is a secretary. This computer is _____.

2 Anne has two children. _____ names are Tom and Harry.

3 Is this Jenny's pen? No it is _____.

4 Hi Lloyd, is this _____ dictionary?

5 Have some cake. It is for _____ birthday.

 Let's write

1 Prepare to write a paragraph about the picture. Use the adjectives in the word box and the questions below to help you make notes.

Word box

big   warm
noisy   colourful
quiet   dirty
beautiful

Example:
What is the place?
It is a **beautiful** park.

Review and assessment 1

1 Where is it? It is in _____.

2 What can you do and see there? You can _____.

3 Who works there? Many people work at the park such as _____.

4 How would you describe it? There are some colourful swings and _____.

5 What do you like about it? It is great because _____.

2 Write the paragraph about the picture. When you finish, check your spelling, grammar and punctuation.

_____
_____
_____
_____
_____
_____
_____

Term 3 Unit 1 Review and assessment 2

 Speaking and listening

Remember ☆☆☆

Use the **present continuous** to describe events that are happening in front of you.

For example: *Two children **are** build**ing** sand castles. They **are** us**ing** their bucket and spade.*

1. Prepare to talk to your partner. Look at the picture of the beach and make notes under the headings.

People	Clothes	Action
two children – a little girl and boy	girl: red hat, boy: red swimming shorts	building sand castles

Review and assessment 2

2. Work with your partner. Take turns to describe the picture. Use the present continuous to describe what is happening now. Use the questions below to help you.
   - Who are the people?
   - What are they wearing?
   - What is happening at the beach?
   - What are people doing?

Example:
There are two children, a little girl and a little boy. The girl is wearing a red hat; the boy is wearing red swimming shorts. They are building sand castles.

Word builder

1. Where are these words in the picture above? Write the words on the picture to show where they are.

Word box

sun	spade
sea	sun hat
sand	beach ball
bucket	ice cream

Remember ☆☆☆

We use words called **adjectives** to describe people, places and objects. For example: *Jamaica is* **beautiful**.

2. Work with a partner. Describe the picture using adjectives from the words below. For example: *The little girl is eating a* **delicious** *ice cream. It is a* **hot**, **sunny** *day.*

Word box

small	skinny	delicious	hot
big	fat	tasty	sunny
little	thin	sweet	windy
tall	short	salty	cool

325

Let's read

1. Choose the best heading from the box for texts A to D and write them in the space.

Word box

Farm   Beach   Carnival   Park

Places in your town

A _____

This is the place we go to walk, play, run, meet friends and sometimes have picnics. Children love this place because they can play on slides, roundabouts and swings. People often bring their dogs here to enjoy a run, play "catch the ball" and have fun.

B _____

In the streets there is Jamaican food for you to try. You can hear traditional Jamaican music, from Bob Marley and even Usain Bolt. You can see happy faces everywhere. People dance and really enjoy themselves.

C _____

This is a place we go to relax, have fun and spend time with friends and family. It can be noisy with children playing or sometimes quiet when the sun is setting. This place is usually busy during the weekends and holiday times. Flying kites, swimming, playing handball and surfing are popular sports at this place.

D _____

This is a piece of land used to grow plants and raise animals for food. Animals such as cows, sheep, goats and chickens live here. The people that work here have an important job because everyone needs food.

Review and assessment 2

Grammar builder

Remember ☆☆☆

A **simple sentence** is a group of words with a subject or a plural subject and a main verb.
The word *and* helps joins parts of a plural subject together.
For example: *My mother and father go to the market every Saturday.*

1. Choose words to make a plural subject and to complete the sentences. Do not forget to add the personal pronoun *my* if it is needed.

Example:
My family and I usually go to the park for a walk.

Word box

nurses	father	aunty	doctors	my
mother	sister	uncle	students	family
teachers	brother	friend	I	

1. _____ and _____ fly kites at the beach in our summer holidays.

2. _____ and _____ work in hospitals.

3. _____ and _____ prepare dinner for the family.

4. _____ and _____ go to school every week.

5. _____ and _____ buy me presents for my birthday.

2. Now write your own sentence using a plural subject.

_____

Let's write

1 Write a short text describing a place you would go to, such as a school or a hospital, <u>but do not write the name of the place</u>.

Use the questions below to help you and look at the texts on the "Let's read" lesson to guide you. When you finish, check your spelling, grammar and punctuation.

1 Where is it? This place is in _____.

2 What can you do and see there? At this place you can _____.

3 How would you describe it? This place is _____.

4 What do you like about it? I like / do not like this place because _____.

_____

_____

_____

_____